Advance Prai
Gray Matters: 100 Devot

M000219452

Ray Frazier has provided us with short, insightful and quality devotional thoughts. His inclusion of quotes and prayers from a diverse collection of writers, along with Scripture references, deepens the reading and reflection experience. Well worth one hundred days!

—Rev. B. Leslie Robinson Jr.
Center for Congregational Health
Winston-Salem, North Carolina

My mother was an avid reader of devotional materials until the last day of her ninety-two years. I wish she could have read *Gray Matters*. This book will encourage others to keep growing as long as God allows them to keep going. Ray Frazier scores 100 for his 100 devotionals for aging adults!

—Ronald S. Cava, D.Min.
Senior Minister, First Baptist Church
Henderson, North Carolina

Drawing on decades of pastoral ministry, Ray Frazier uses his considerable wit and wisdom to mine the scriptures for easily applicable insights for retirees. Each line rests on his fundamental belief that every season in life is valuable and rich with opportunity. *Gray Matters* will make you smile, reflect and hear God's word in fresh, new ways. I'm so looking forward to sharing it with the retirees in our church!

—Rev. Alicia Davis Porterfield
Interim pastor and former eldercare chaplain

Smyth & Helwys Publishing, Inc.
6316 Peake Road
Macon, Georgia 31210-3960
1-800-747-3016
©2015 by Edwin Ray Frazier
All rights reserved.

Library of Congress Cataloging-in-Publication Data

Frazier, Edwin Ray, 1945- author.
One hundred devotions for the aging / By Edwin Ray Frazier.
pages cm
ISBN 978-1-57312-837-7 (pbk. : alk. paper)
1. Older people--Prayers and devotions. I. Title.
BV4580.F69 2015
242'.65--dc23

2015028102

EDWIN RAY FRAZIER

GRAY**MATTERS**

100 Devotions *for the* Aging

Also by Edwin Ray Frazier

The First Hundred Days:
100 Devotions for New Christians

Dedication

For my immediate family, all of whom were or are in the category of "aging adults."

In grateful memory of my parents Bob and Violet Frazier, and my brothers Earle and Syl.

In love and appreciation for my sisters Thelma, Barnes, Pearle, and Myrtas, and my brother Roy.

I'm thankful that I am who I am because of them.

Acknowledgments

Several aging individuals have mentored me along the way.

In my first full time pastorate, a Methodist minister, Rev. Henry O'Brien, and I served in the small Georgia town of Bethlehem. He was concluding his life's work; I was beginning mine. He helped me get my head back on straight a few times.

In Roanoke, Virginia, Dr. Lynn Dickerson was a prominent Virginia pastor who had retired in the congregation that called me as their pastor. He asked the pulpit committee to bring me by his house. In my early thirties, I was scared to death when he left the committee in the living room and took me back to the kitchen. He said, "Brother Frazier, I just want you to know that if these people call you as their pastor, and if you accept, I know how to let you be their pastor, and I will do that." Not only was he true to his word, but his friendship and counsel were invaluable.

In Woodstock, Virginia, in my second Intentional Interim Pastorate, Rev. Richard Moyers was and still is a wise and dear friend, confidante, and encourager.

It's interesting what sticks in your mind. As a young pastor I went to visit Mamie Williams one day. She had lived her life and was still able to keep house by herself, with the help of her devoted son, who lived in the same town. We sat in her small living room by a large window. One of the most unassuming individuals I can recall, she had a remarkably contagious peace. I thought about our country's social turmoils that she had lived through, and about the fact that surely she had had her own turmoils as well. As we talked I looked out at a walnut tree and watched two squirrels play more leisurely than most squirrels do. Even they seemed to be at peace.

The Lord has always seemed to have someone older and wiser than I nearby, to hold my hand and walk with me. Sometimes our interaction was brief and seemingly superficial; at other times it was deeper and lasted longer. In addition to my family members named in the dedication, these other aging individuals also played significant roles in who I am. Thereby they also played significant roles in making these devotions possible.

Contents

Preface

This work is presented in the assumption that most seniors are active to some degree. The devotions are not an expert's pronouncements about what you ought to do; they are a fellow traveler's suggestions about what we would all do well to consider.

They are biblically based, each with a focal text (or two) and three other passages that may prompt further reflection and insight. Each devotion treats a topic. In the case of those about Bible personalities, the topic relates to that character but is not always the most obvious or definitive topic for that individual.

The approach throughout is spiritual, carried out in view of two Bible passages. Galatians 5:22-23 describes or identifies the fruit of the spirit in terms of nine virtues, attitudes, or spirits. In Matthew 5:21-48, part of Jesus' Sermon on the Mount, six times Jesus quotes a religious rule or law, and each time he supersedes it with a religious virtue, attitude, or spirit. These two passages suggest that God looks on our inner spirits more than our outward actions. In these devotions I have aimed to take the same spiritual focus.

After five introductory devotions about basic matters of Christian faith, thirty-five devotions treat thirty-five Christian virtues. The remaining sixty take us through a gallery of Bible characters, each presenting a truth in the conviction that we can glean real life lessons best from the biblical record of real people who lived real lives.

These devotions average about 465 words each—a length that is appropriate for quiet time over morning coffee, a moment before bedtime to ponder God's work in your day, or anytime between. Choose the time that best serves your schedule, even if it changes from day to day.

I hope these one hundred devotions will engage readers sufficiently to help them see God's presence more clearly—for the next one hundred days and beyond.

Some prayers are the works of other writers and speakers. Some are my own prayers. This variety should give readers a broader scope both in praying and in improving their own prayer habits. About ninety percent of the material is positive. However, some truths are presented negatively, as in the devotions about Pharaoh, Judas, and Pilate.

The topics and discussions grew out of my forty years in the pastoral ministry. I found most of the Quotes to Remember through online research, and references are included in the Notes section. Several Bible translations are used and are always indicated.

Introduction

Happiness and fulfillment depend on relating appropriately to our current life stage. The youth who wants to be viewed as instantly wise and experienced is likely to meet with disappointment. On the other hand, the teen who studies and lays the groundwork for self-respect in adulthood is likely to be content with who she is and who she is becoming. As the decades pass, one person stumbles painfully along from frustration to frustration. The other ages gracefully.

At every stage in life, many people find their highest joy and satisfaction by investing in something bigger than themselves. God forever calls followers forward, onward and upward. God is always a few steps ahead of us, beckoning.

These devotions reflect on relating biblical truth appropriately to those called "seniors," "elderly," "retirees," or "the aging." I draw from two kinds of sources. One source is the spirits or attitudes that the Christian Scriptures hold up as godly. The other source is the wisdom we find in contemplating the lives of biblical characters. Like the clothes we wear, these truths are needed at every life stage from early childhood on. And like the clothes we wear, these truths have an appropriately different appearance at different life stages.

My goal in these pages is to offer biblical perspectives that give guidance and motivation to aging individuals so that we may choose to invest in something bigger than ourselves. We have not yet outgrown the upward call of our God.

For some, this investment may be a first-time experience. For others, it will be a reviewing and renewing of commitments made to the Lord decades ago. May the Lord of all life inspire our hearts as we meditate on how to meet the passing years with Christlike grace and dignity.

First Things First

A book of Christian devotions appropriately begins with some basic thoughts about what it means to be a Christian. These five devotions present five perspectives that are foundational to a good relationship with the Lord and to a Christian life:

Following Christ
Servanthood
Stewardship
Christian Community
Discipleship

1 Following Christ
Choosing to Be a Christian

*"Come, follow me," Jesus said.
(Matt 4:19, NIV)*

Choosing to be a Christian means I have recognized that my natural outlook is selfish, turned inward. We call this outlook "original sin," and every human being is born with it. Living as a Christian also means that I choose Christ as the one who can set me free for a more abundant life, enabling me to live for higher and holier purposes than what I can get or do for myself. My life's direction gets revamped and reengineered through Christ.

We've heard numerous explanations of how to become a Christian, also known as "the plan of salvation." In some way, each explanation calls on the individual to admit his natural selfishness and to give himself over to Jesus Christ as Savior and Deliverer.

Just as the moment comes when we sign a dotted line to take on a mortgage, or a moment comes when we say "I do" to commit to another person in marriage, there is also a watershed moment when we confirm that Jesus is our Lord and Master. For some it's a spectacular moment of excitement and emotion. For others it's a calm and quiet decision. However it comes about, we can't get the mortgage without the signing or the marriage without the promise, and we can't be Christians without coming to the moment of decision. Admiring the mortgage arrangement is not the same as taking out a mortgage. Admiring a fiancé or fiancée is not the same as committing to a lifelong partnership. Likewise, surrendering to live as the Lord directs us to live is much more than admiring Jesus.

We cannot know all that today's decisions will mean tomorrow. We make choices based on faith. With a mortgage, with marriage, and with religious faith, we sign up for what we hope will be. We say, "I do, I will." We spend a reasonable amount of time shopping around, and then we decide. Today is a good day to decide for Christ. If you haven't done that, will you do it now?

A Quote to Remember

The moment you have a self at all, there is a possibility of putting yourself first, wanting to be the center, wanting to be God, in fact. That was the sin of Satan: and that was the sin he taught the human race.[1] (C. S. Lewis)

Think on These Things

Trust in the LORD with all your heart; do not depend on your own understanding. (Prov 3:5, NLT)

For everyone has sinned; we all fall short of God's glorious standard. (Rom 3:23, NLT)

If the earthly tent we live in is destroyed, we have a building from God, an eternal house in heaven. For we live by faith, not by sight. (2 Cor 5:1, 7, NIV)

Prayer

Heavenly Father, I want to sign up. I want to escape the chains of my selfish nature. I want to be set free to be higher and better, free to serve you rather than myself. Forgive my sinfulness, I pray, and recreate me as your child for all eternity. Amen.

2 Servanthood
Growing a Servant's Heart

You do not belong to yourself, for
God bought you with a high price.
(1 Cor 6:19-20, NLT)

The idea of slavery or even servanthood is not as familiar in the twenty-first century as it was in Bible times. We have to make an effort to comprehend the biblical truth about it. In those days, slaves and servants were bought and sold, and that custom was a familiar and accurate illustration of the Lord's ownership of those who followed him. With some thought, we may find that servanthood is still a useful idea and image in our time.

By our free will and choice, God owns us. We live for him and for his purposes. We serve him. We carry out his wishes as best we understand them, rather than fulfilling our own self-centered wishes.

In deciding to follow Christ, we turn away from sin and self-ishness. I am no longer the most important person in my life; God is. Jesus said that the greatest commandment is that we love God, and the next most important commandment follows close on the heels of the first: we love our neighbor. Therefore we have become servants to the will of God. By serving God, we serve others.

We are proud of our independence, and when rightly understood, that's not a bad thing. God created us independent in the sense that no human person owns us or makes our decisions. But in our relationship to God, it is his desire that we place ourselves in his service. He becomes the master. We become his servants, voluntary slaves to his directions for living.

A Quote to Remember

To maintain a joyful family requires much from both the parents and the children. Each member of the family has to become, in a special way, the servant of the others and share their burdens. Each one must show concern, not only for his or her own life, but also for the lives of the other members of the family: their needs, their hopes, their ideals.[2] (Pope John Paul II)

Think on These Things

Jesus . . . said, "You know that the rulers of the Gentiles lord it over them, and their great ones exercise authority over them. It shall not be so among you. But whoever would be great among you must be your servant, and whoever would be first among you must be your slave, even as the Son of Man came not to be served but to serve." (Matt 20:25-28, ESV)

Prayer

Create in me a servant's heart, O Lord! Please help me to follow your example of servanthood. Create in me a heart of humility that will not allow fame and status to get in the way of service, just as you did not allow equality with God to prevent you from service. Lord, please help me not only to look and sound like a servant, but to actually take the role of a servant, as you did. Lord, please make me a servant like you! Amen.[3]

3 Stewardship
Managing Our Possessions

It is required of stewards that one be
found trustworthy. (1 Cor 4:2, NASB)

The Bible's outlook is that human beings are stewards or managers of God's possessions. Our homes, our bank accounts, and even our bodies belong to the Lord. We manage them for him according to his directions.

The Lord says, "Every animal of the forest is mine, and the cattle on a thousand hills. The world is mine, and all that is in it" (Ps 50:10, 12, NIV). King David also recognized that "the earth is the LORD's, and everything in it, the world, and all who live in it" (Ps 24:1, NIV).

Suppose that, in the next newscast, we learn about someone sent to prison for embezzling or misappropriating funds. This person was entrusted with company money and acted like it belonged to him. He used the trust for his own purposes rather than for the company's purposes. According to the law, and according to the Lord, that's a crime. Each employee's fulfillment is found in relation to the good stewardship of all members of the company.

Stewards seek to understand the Lord's purposes and invest their lives for those purposes. The Christmas angel said that God is a God of peace and good will (Luke 2:14, KJV). The story of this angelic visit to the shepherds is one of several Bible texts that define God's purposes for our lives. We find fulfillment as we learn to be good stewards of what God has given us.

A Quote to Remember

A checkbook is a theological document; it will tell you who and what you worship. If a person gets his attitude toward money straight, it will help straighten out almost every other area of his life.[4] (Billy Graham)

Think on These Things

Behold, all souls are Mine; the soul of the father as well as the soul of the son is Mine. (Ezek 18:4, NASB)

"The silver is mine and the gold is mine," declares the Lord Almighty. (Hag 2:8, NIV)

For none of us lives for ourselves alone, and none of us dies for ourselves alone. If we live, we live for the Lord; and if we die, we die for the Lord. So, whether we live or die, we belong to the Lord. (Rom 14:7-8, NIV)

Prayer

Praise be to you, LORD, the God of our father Israel, from everlasting to everlasting. Yours, LORD, is the greatness and the power and the glory and the majesty and the splendor, for everything in heaven and earth is yours. Yours, LORD, is the kingdom; you are exalted as head over all. Wealth and honor come from you; you are the ruler of all things. In your hands are strength and power to exalt and give strength to all. Now, our God, we give you thanks, and praise your glorious name. (1 Chron 29:10-14, NIV)

4 **Christian Community**
Belonging to a Church

They devoted themselves to the apostles' teaching and to fellowship, to the breaking of bread and to prayer. Every day they continued to meet together in the temple courts. They broke bread in their homes and ate together with glad and sincere hearts, and the Lord added to their number daily those who were being saved. (Acts 2:42, 46, 48, NIV)

In any area of the country, the best citizens have a sense of community: they think of themselves as individual parts of a larger whole. They work for the good of the community. In any area of the country, the worst citizens do not have a sense of community. They think of themselves as free agents. They work for their own good, even at the expense of everyone else around them.

God's people are called to community. We need each other for friendship and encouragement, for challenge and restraint. We need to belong to a "household of faith" (Gal 6:10, ESV). The Bible presents a picture of a family atmosphere in the early church. Certainly, they had their peculiar and irritating personalities just as we do. Still, they belonged.

It's childish and unbiblical to think that we can live for the Lord in isolation from others. Christianity is a relational religion: it is about how we relate to God and to others.

National citizenship affords us many privileges and also requires some "belonging" activities like paying taxes and abiding by the law. That dynamic carries over into church membership.

Be a part of a local church, a spiritual community with a unique set of weaknesses and strengths, warts and blemishes, joys and rewards, failures and shortcomings. The church is our Lord's provision to meet our need to be part of a larger whole, to fulfill our sense of community.

A Quote to Remember

The little typed reminder on train tickets, "No good if detached," applies to those who number themselves with the redeemed: no good if detached from the body of believers. God has no Christians Anonymous.[5] (Roy McClain)

Think on These Things

As we have opportunity, let us do good to everyone, and especially to those who are of the household of faith. (Gal 6:10, ESV)

God placed all things under his [Jesus'] feet and appointed him to be head over everything for the church, which is his body. (Eph 1:22-23, NIV)

Let us not neglect our meeting together, as some people do. (Heb 10:25, NLT)

Prayer

Lord I thank you for the church that is your body, and for my local congregation that is one manifestation of your body. Bless our leaders and all who worship together there, I pray. Grant me grace to act redemptively toward others' warts and blemishes, and to be humble about my own shortcomings. Make me a point of strength in my church. Amen.

5 Discipleship
Growing as We Age

There is so much more I want to tell you, but you can't bear it now. When the Spirit of truth comes, he will guide you into all truth. (John 16:12-13, NLT)

Jesus spoke these words to his disciples the night before he was crucified. He had taught them personally for three years, but they still had so much more to learn. He was not limited in his ability to teach; they were limited in their ability to learn. But they would grow.

One valid perspective on discipleship is that it is a life-long process of growth. Every serious Bible student has experienced the discovery of something new and invigorating in a passage they have read numerous times. As time passes, God's Spirit broadens and increases our understanding, or at least that's the way God intends for discipleship to work.

Rash, brash Peter grew spiritually to the point that he wrote his New Testament letters, giving evidence that he had become sensitive and tactful. John, the Son of Thunder, grew spiritually to the point where he wrote his letters full of love and became "The Apostle of Love."

God does not change. But as the tiny cup of our tiny understanding grows, we comprehend more about who he is and who he wants us to be. Today there is much more that the Lord desires for us to comprehend, but we can't grasp it right now, the same way that a child cannot grasp adult realities for another fifteen or twenty years.

Once we learn the multiplication tables, we've got them. That never changes. All we need is a little reminder or refresher from time to time. In spiritual things, however, the sun is forever rising on a new day, with new truths to learn as we follow our Lord in discipleship.

A Quote to Remember

Growing old is mandatory. Growing up is optional.[6] (Cindy Gerard)

Think on These Things

When I was a child, I used to speak like a child, think like a child, reason like a child; when I became a man, I did away with childish things. (1 Cor 13:11, NASB)

Speaking the truth in love, we are to grow up in all aspects into Him who is the head, even Christ. (Eph 4:15, NASB)

Grow in the grace and knowledge of our Lord and Savior Jesus Christ. To Him be the glory, both now and to the day of eternity. (2 Pet 3:18, NASB)

Prayer

Heavenly Father, thank you for allowing many of us to walk with you, called by your name, for many years. Forgive us for acting like children, for talking like new Christians, for being satisfied with faith that's still in diapers. Thank you for the Bible's real men and women who, to their dying day, were pressing forward in discipleship. May we follow in their footsteps, we pray. Amen.

The Fruit of the Spirit

The next ten devotions grow out of Galatians 5:22-23, which names the nine virtues of the Spirit: Love, Joy, Peace, Patience, Kindness, Goodness, Faithfulness, Gentleness, and Self-control. These are the inner traits of the heart that authenticate the outer works of the hands. They are the evidence that prove a genuine faith. Without them, confessions of faith are empty.

This is the direction of our striving, our spiritual goal for personal development. This is what it means to be Christlike.

6 Ageless Attitudes
Proving Our Identity

The fruit of the Spirit is love, joy,
peace, patience, kindness, goodness,
faithfulness, gentleness, self-control.
(Gal 5:22-23, NASB)

In Matthew 21:23-31, the religious leaders try to embarrass Jesus in conversation. Their spirits, or attitudes, are harsh and judgmental. Jesus says that some prostitutes will get into the kingdom of heaven before the leaders will get in. Of course, these first-century counterparts of preachers and deacons think they are the most righteous people alive. But church membership and whatever theology we embrace mean nothing in comparison to our spirits. Our attitudes are who we are.

We identify Christlike spirits, attitudes, and virtues in the thirty-five meditations that follow. These are the proofs of our Christian identity. We begin with the nine virtues in Galatians 5:22-23.

At the checkout counter, the clerk may ask for photo identification. If we look like the picture, then the clerk is satisfied that we are indeed who we say we are. But if a short, fat, bald man presents a picture of a tall, muscular, athletic guy, the clerk is suspicious.

Paul presents a nine-point picture of a child of God. If we look like the picture, then we are indeed God's children. Let us welcome these virtues, allowing them to intertwine and seep into our spirits.

A Quote to Remember

I like your Christ, but I do not like your Christians. They are not like him.[7] (Mahatma Gandhi)

Think on These Things

You, however, are not in the realm of the flesh but are in the realm of the Spirit, if indeed the Spirit of God lives in you. And if anyone does not have the Spirit of Christ, they do not belong to Christ. (Rom 8:9, NIV)

Now the Lord is that Spirit: and where the Spirit of the Lord is, there is liberty. (2 Cor 3:17, KJV)

The fruit of the Spirit is in all goodness and righteousness and truth. (Eph 5:9, KJV)

───────⊗⊗⊗───────

Prayer

Lord of love, joy, and peace, grow me in your likeness, I pray. God of patience, kindness, and goodness, live in me and through me, I pray. Spirit of faithfulness, gentleness, and self-control, bear your fruit in my interactions with others, I pray. I desire above all else to be like you.

In the meditations of coming days, guide the paths of my thoughts, that they may increasingly mold and make me in your image. I surrender to you now all that stands in the way of my becoming what you desire me to be, in order that I may accomplish the service to which you have called me. Take away every part of me that is not Christlike, I pray. In their place, plant and nurture the fruit of your Spirit until there is room for nothing else. Amen.

7 Love
Wanting the Best for Others

For God so loved the world that he
gave his one and only Son.
(John 3:16, NIV)

There's nothing wrong with moonlight and roses and "falling" in love. Biblical love, however, is more often a resolution, a decision, a commitment to want the best for others always, regardless of how they treat us. We speak and act in their best interests without regard to whether or not they deserve our love. Love is about who we are; it's not about how we're treated.

It's unfortunate that we use the same word for our love of a sports team that we use for our love of God. Those two meanings are light years apart. It's confusing to speak of loving our neighbor and also of loving chocolate. Biblical love is not about our likes and dislikes; it's about the way we choose to relate to others.

Therefore, if a neighbor needs encouragement or rebuke or food or a constant friend, we choose always to seek her welfare. If an irritating person needs acceptance or correction, we resolve to say and do what is in his best interests. We try always to comprehend how we may speak and act in order to bring about what's best for others. That's what it means to have God's kind of love.

A Quote to Remember

And you must love him, ere to you
He will seem worthy of your love.[8] (William Wordsworth)

Think on These Things

Let us love one another. (1 John 4:7, NIV)

"Of all the commandments, which is the most important?" "The most important one," answered Jesus, "is this: 'Hear, O Israel: The Lord our God, the Lord is one. Love the Lord your God with all your heart and with all your soul and with all your mind and with all your strength.' The second is this: 'Love your neighbor as yourself.' There is no commandment greater than these." (Mark 12:28-31, NIV)

Do nothing from rivalry or conceit, but in humility count others more significant than yourselves. Let each of you look not only to his own interests, but also to the interests of others. (Phil 2:3-4, ESV)

Prayer

For My Friends

Lord, thank You for friends
Who warm my life with their smiles,
Who make life worthwhile,
Who carry me when courage fails
And comfort me when I am sad.
Thank You for their honesty
When I cannot be honest with myself,
For letting me grow in my own time,
For respecting my feelings.
In a world where love seems lost
My friends love me.
Thank You Lord for all of them.
Amen.[9]

8 Joy
Choosing to Rejoice

Rejoice in the Lord always. I will say it again: Rejoice! (Phil 4:4, NIV)

There are days when this command seems useless at best. At worst, it can seem to add insult to injury. We've all had a witch's brew of pain and turmoil. On such days, how could we possibly rejoice? The key, of course, is the will to look for something to be glad about.

God does not ask us to be unrealistic and ignore heartbreak. To any situation, however, we can add a griping spirit or a positive spirit. The griping spirit seldom wins. Every winner in every game looks for something positive, something to rejoice in and to capitalize on.

We rejoice "in the Lord." Every blessing we have comes from God. That viewpoint enables us to rejoice.

"We have so much to be thankful for." My mother said this frequently. We weren't wealthy; we experienced illness, tragedy, and the death of young family members. I also remember my sister saying once, "There's enough trouble to drive you crazy if you just sit down and think about it." So today shall we think about our troubles, or shall we be thankful and joyful?

Rejoicing is not about our circumstances. It's about our choice to rejoice.

Our text today is from one of the Apostle Paul's warmest letters. But he wrote it from the confines of prison. He had a great many painful realities to drive him crazy. Instead, he chose to practice his preaching. He made the choice that we can make: the choice to rejoice.

A Quote to Remember

A merry heart goes all the day,
Your sad [heart] tires in a mile.[10] (William Shakespeare)

Think on These Things

I am overwhelmed with joy in the LORD my God! For he has dressed me with the clothing of salvation and draped me in a robe of righteousness. I am like a bridegroom in his wedding suit or a bride with her jewels. (Isa 61:10, NLT)

For the Kingdom of God is not a matter of what we eat or drink, but of living a life of goodness and peace and joy in the Holy Spirit. (Rom 14:17, NLT)

You love him even though you have never seen him. Though you do not see him now, you trust him; and you rejoice with a glorious, inexpressible joy. (1 Peter 1:8, NLT)

Prayer

Giver of every good and perfect gift, I bow before you as the source of every joy in my life—past, present, and future. And I thank you for those joys: for kind hands that have held mine in the past and that hold them today; for kind hearts that have cared for me in the past and those who care today. And thank you for the city not made with hands, toward which I live. In your time, O Lord, bring me safely into your presence, that I may know the blessing of being with you forever. Amen.

9 **Peace**
Turning Away from "The Big I"

The mind governed by the flesh is death, but the mind governed by the Spirit is life and peace. (Rom 8:6, NIV)

The "mind governed by the flesh" is our sinful, selfish nature. The "mind governed by the Spirit" is our God-given, unselfish nature. The King James Bible says "to be carnally minded is death, but to be spiritually minded is life and peace."

The Bible recognizes an unbreakable connection between spiritual priorities and peace: the path to peace is living by giving first importance to spiritual things. This eternal rule holds for individuals, families, groups of all kinds, and nations. It is as dependable as gravity.

The most understandable accurate definition of sin is selfishness. We could write paragraph definitions or even volumes, but essentially sin is selfishness. Giving first importance to spiritual things means turning our life's focus away from "the big I" and out toward others. God's grace in our hearts replaces selfishness with selflessness. This about-face turns us away from the world's rat pit of quarrels and toward life and peace.

As an apple proves the tree to be an apple tree, so peace is one aspect of the fruit that proves that God's Spirit lives in us and is at work in us.

A Quote to Remember

The storm was raging. The sea was beating against the rocks in huge, dashing waves. The lightning was flashing, the thunder was roaring, the wind was blowing; but the little bird was asleep in the crevice of the rock, its head serenely under its wing, sound asleep. That is peace: to be able to rest serenely in the storm![11] (Billy Graham)

Think on These Things

You will keep in perfect peace those whose minds are steadfast, because they trust in you. Trust in the LORD forever, for the LORD, the LORD himself, is the Rock eternal. (Isa 26:3-4, NIV)

In peace I will lie down and sleep, for you alone, LORD, make me dwell in safety. (Ps 4:8, NIV)

And suddenly there was with the angel a multitude of the heavenly host praising God, and saying, "Glory to God in the highest, and on earth peace, good will toward men." (Luke 2:13-14, KJV)

Prayer

Almighty God, we bless you for the life you have given. We praise you for your grace and peace. We thank you for your faithfulness to us in the face of our unfaithfulness to you. Forgive our selfishness, we pray, that we may be at peace within ourselves and thereby become peacemakers in a troubled world. Work peace in and through us until the Christmas angel's announcement comes to fruition: "peace and good will on earth." Amen.

10 Patience
Enduring and Persevering

So be patient, brothers, until the coming of the Lord. See how the farmer waits for the precious crop from his land, being patient with it until it receives the fall and the spring rains. (Jas 5:7, ISV)

"Patience" is a great Bible word. A moment's thought on our text calls attention to the great difference in the way the word was used in New Testament times and the way we often use it today. By "patience," we often mean sitting and waiting, hoping, wishing, doing nothing. Anyone who knows anything about growing flowers, vegetables, or farm crops realizes that a farmer's patience is full of plowing, planting, cultivating, and fighting weeds and insects. A farmer's patience, and the patience of a child of God, is *work*.

Biblical patience is perseverance, stick-to-itiveness, endurance.

It is true that waiting on the Lord has its place. Such waiting is commanded in a few places in the Bible (Ps 27:14; Mic 7:7; Mark 15:43; Rom 8:23-25).

But in this verse, God's word through James to the original readers and to us is not about waiting. It's about being faithful in every way we possibly can. It's about praying for strength and wisdom to do God's will and God's work rather than praying that God will do it all.

A Quote to Remember

Patience is not passive: on the contrary it is active; it is concentrated strength. There is one form of hope which is never unwise, and which certainly does not diminish with the increase of knowledge. In that form it changes its name, and we call it patience.[12] (Edward G. Bulwer-Lytton)

Think on These Things

Be still before the LORD and wait patiently for him; do not fret when people succeed in their ways, when they carry out their wicked schemes. Refrain from anger and turn from wrath; do not fret; it leads only to evil. For those who are evil will be destroyed, but those who hope in the LORD will inherit the land. (Ps 37:7-9, NIV)

If we look forward to something we don't yet have, we must wait patiently and confidently. (Rom 8:25, NLT)

But let patience have her perfect work, that ye may be perfect and entire, wanting nothing. (Jas 1:4, KJV)

Prayer

Lord of patience and endurance, I come to you as the One who cares about me and desires to strengthen me for today and all the days ahead. I worship you as my reason for living. I seek your grace to persevere through the challenges facing me now and the decisions that must be made in Christian integrity. Grant me your patience, O Lord, I pray. In Jesus' name. Amen.

11 Kindness
Creating a Habitat for Righteousness

Since God chose you to be the holy people he loves, you must clothe yourselves with tenderhearted mercy, kindness, humility, gentleness, and patience. Make allowance for each other's faults, and forgive anyone who offends you. Remember, the Lord forgave you, so you must forgive others. (Col 3:12-13, NLT)

Kindness creates an environment in which all goodness, peace, and righteousness flourish. Kindness destroys the environment in which evil, hatred, and violence prosper.

The Bengal tiger is one of the most beautiful creatures the Lord ever created. It is an endangered species, however, and not only because of poaching. Human progress has destroyed much of its habitat. As civilization creates community environments in which people prosper, we also destroy the environments and habitats in which many beautiful species flourish.

Every kind word or deed helps create a habitat for good and helps destroy the habitat for evil.

Some dentists explain that brushing our teeth may kill a few bacteria. But the primary benefit of brushing is that it destroys the environment, the habitat, in which bacteria thrive, and it creates an environment in which teeth remain strong.

Kindness works that way. All the good and godly qualities that we desire in our lives and in the lives of others are fed and nourished by the kind words we say today. All the evil and destructive qualities that we spurn are discouraged by the kind deeds we do today. Give someone the heartening experience of seeing what kindness looks like.

Today and every day, let us exude kindness. In this way, we bring blessing upon ourselves and on others as well.

A Quote to Remember
Kindness gives birth to kindness.[13] (Sophocles)

Think on These Things
Those who are kind benefit themselves, but the cruel bring ruin on themselves. (Prov 11:17, NIV)

To sum up, all of you be harmonious, sympathetic, brotherly, kindhearted, and humble in spirit. (1 Pet 3:8, NASB)

Get rid of all bitterness, rage and anger, brawling and slander, along with every form of malice. Be kind and compassionate to one another, forgiving each other, just as in Christ God forgave you. (Eph 4:29-32, NIV)

Prayer
Heavenly Father, thank you for your unchanging and eternal loving kindness to me, and for those who have been kind to me along the way. Grow in me a heart for kindness, that increasingly I may recognize opportunities to speak and act in ways that please you. Amen.

12 **Goodness**
Doing the Right Thing

Jesus went around doing good.
(Acts 10:38)

Christ has left us an example, that
we should follow in his footsteps.
(from 1 Pet 2:21)

Some powerful and life-changing truths come to us in words so simple, so familiar, that we overlook their importance. It's like the beautiful rose by the door where we enter and exit several times a day. Our attention is given to new things, things that we did not see yesterday and are not likely to look for tomorrow unless we have a change of heart.

Nevertheless, goodness is one of our lives' most important paths. We must choose this path; we do not find it by accident.

It's easy enough to be good, to do the right thing, when life has showered us with goodness and our cups overflow with pleasantness. We do well to consider that Jesus experienced a great deal that challenged his choice to do good, to be a good person. His opponents constantly accused him falsely and sought to entrap him in public conversation. He was misrepresented at every turn and misunderstood often by those closest to him. It was not easy for Jesus to go around doing good. Ultimately his generation's self-appointed guardians of religion tortured him to death on a Roman cross. Still, his goodness shone brightly in his prayer, "Father, forgive them because they don't know what they're doing" (Luke 23:34).

A Quote to Remember

It's the action, not the fruit of the action, that's important. You have to do the right thing. It may not be in your power, may not be in your time, that there'll be any fruit. But that doesn't mean you stop doing the right thing. You may never know what results come from your action. But if you do nothing, there will be no result.[14] (Mahatma Gandhi)

Think on These Things

This is a trustworthy saying, and I want you to insist on these teachings so that all who trust in God will devote themselves to doing good. These teachings are good and beneficial for everyone. (Titus 3:8, NLT)

Let us not become weary in doing good, for at the proper time we will reap a harvest if we do not give up. (Gal 6:9, NIV)

Therefore, to one who knows the right thing to do and does not do it, to him it is sin. (Jas 4:17, NASB)

Prayer

O Infinite God, of life, goodness, and generous
love, I dedicate my heart, my life, to you.
Help me to cherish all human life,
and do the good you want me to do.
Make me a loving example of your generous love,
and a blessing to everyone I see.
May your goodness be fully in us, and in all that we
think, and say and do.[15]

13 Faithfulness
Living with Honesty and Diligence

Well done, good and faithful servant.
(Matt 25:21, NIV)

Faithfulness appears in slightly different forms in various Bible texts. In Jesus' parable of the three servants, we see that faithfulness is honesty, diligence, and the servant attitude. (Other synonyms are trustworthy, reliable, dependable, unchanging.) A master left three servants in charge of three amounts of money. Later, when he called the three for a reckoning, two of them had used the money entrusted to them to earn more for their master. The third had buried the money entrusted to him, and he gave back to the master the same amount he had received in trust. The master called the first two good and faithful. The third, however, he called "wicked and lazy." Only the first two honestly accepted their responsibility, carried it out diligently, and did so in the understanding that they were serving their master.

The master, of course, represents God, and the servants represent us. We are responsible to accept the teachings of Scripture as God's commands, to carry them out diligently, and to do so in the understanding that we are not our own; we serve our divine master.

There will be a day of reckoning. All of us do well to live so as to hear the Lord's "well done, good and faithful servant" when our time comes.

A Quote to Remember

Mother Teresa of Calcutta spent her life for poor people. Perhaps it's more appropriate to say that she invested her life that way.

Her consuming passion took the forms both of personal sacrifice, and efforts to sway society to care for the poor. There are several versions of the events that led to her famous quote. One is that someone asked her if she realized that she could be successful in any of several careers. To which she responded, "God has not called me to be successful; He has called me to be faithful."[16]

Think on These Things

The trustworthy person will get a rich reward, but a person who wants quick riches will get into trouble. (Prov 28:20, NLT)

Moreover it is required in stewards, that a man be found faithful. (1 Cor 4:2, KJV)

If you are faithful in little things, you will be faithful in large ones. But if you are dishonest in little things, you won't be honest with greater responsibilities. (Luke 16:10, NLT)

Prayer

Faithful God, I praise you for who you are, and for your everlasting loving kindnesses to me. Mold and make me more and more, day by day, into your good and faithful servant. Build strong within me the resolution to seek to be a trustworthy servant in your eyes more than to be successful in the world's eyes. O Lord, I surrender this day to you, and I pray for the grace to be honest and diligent in the responsibilities you have entrusted to me. Amen.

14 **Gentleness**
Having Power under the Master's Authority

Be completely humble and gentle; be patient, bearing with one another in love. (Eph 4:2, NIV)

Again the Bible redefines words that are familiar to us. Two words, "gentle" and "meek," have similar meanings: controlled power, directed strength, guided might. How different from the way we use those words to mean weak, powerless, or impotent.

When Scripture encourages us to be gentle, or when Jesus describes himself as gentle (Matt 11:29), we must recall that the meaning is biblical, not modern.

Perhaps you have seen the postcard picture of a dozen German shepherds sitting in a row while a cat meanders by a few feet in front of them. That's biblical gentleness: not weakness, but strength contained and power under control.

From ancient times, we find either of these two words used to describe a wild horse that had been tamed, broken to the saddle or to work under the authority of its master.

The point then, is that God brings direction to our strengths, control to our powerful personalities, guidance to our wild impulses. He does not make his children weak and powerless. When we live under our Master's authority, our speech, actions, and interactions are blessed by the perennially soothing therapy of a gentle nature.

A Quote to Remember

Strong men can always afford to be gentle. Only the weak are intent on "giving as good as they get."[17] (Elbert Hubbard)

Think on These Things

Then Jesus said, "Come to me, all of you who are weary and carry heavy burdens, and I will give you rest. Take my yoke upon you. Let me teach you, because I am humble and gentle, and you will find rest for your souls." (Matt 11:28-29, NLT)

Again I say, don't get involved in foolish, ignorant arguments that only start fights. The Lord's servants must not quarrel but must be kind to everyone. They must be able to teach effectively and be patient with difficult people. They should gently teach those who oppose the truth. (2 Tim 2:23-25, NLT)

If you are asked about your Christian hope, always be ready to explain it. But you must do this in a gentle and respectful way. Keep your conscience clear. (1 Pet 3:15-16, NLT)

Prayer

Gentle Shepherd, control my mind and my spirit today under your authority. Tame my wild impulses and direct my strengths to paths of service to you and to others. Grant me the presence of mind to stay out of foolish and ignorant arguments, and to teach patiently and effectively when you give me the opportunity. In Jesus' name, amen.

15 Self-control
Ruling One's Own Spirit

He that hath no rule over his own spirit is like a city that is broken down, and without walls. (Prov 25:28, KJV)

Self-control is mastery over all our human wants and desires such as sex, greed, revenge, and even chocolate. The King James Bible sometimes translates it as "temperance."

More basically, why is self-control important to begin with? In 1 Corinthians 9:25-27, Paul indicates that he practices self-control to refrain from all that might hamper reaching his divinely assigned goal, carrying out his commission, and bringing the good news of salvation to everyone he can reach. The point is that we need to exercise self-control in order to be and do what the Lord has called us to be and do. When we strike like a cornered rattler, we'll be treated like a snake.

Therefore, we control our speech for divine purposes. A mighty river can be harnessed to provide power to thousands of people, but if it floods it can destroy thousands of acres of land. Similarly, our speech can bless greatly, or it can do great harm. Our divine calling is to bless, not to bring harm. To a significant degree, self-control can determine the seasons of the soul.

Consider self-control in regard to our tempers. Leonardo da Vinci said, "You will never have a greater or lesser dominion than that over yourself . . . a man's success is gauged by his self-mastery; his failure by his self-abandonment. He who cannot establish dominion over himself will have no dominion over others."[18]

A Quote to Remember

I am a spiritual being. After this body is dead, my spirit will soar. I refuse to let what will rot, rule the eternal. I choose self-control. I will be drunk only by joy. I will be impassioned only by my faith. I will be influenced only by God. I will be taught only by Christ. I choose self-control.[19] (Max Lucado)

Think on These Things

He [an overseer] must be hospitable, one who loves what is good, who is self-controlled, upright, holy and disciplined. (Titus 1:8, NIV)

Make every effort to add to your faith goodness; and to goodness, knowledge; and to knowledge, self-control; and to self-control, perseverance; and to perseverance, godliness; and to godliness, mutual affection; and to mutual affection, love. (2 Pet 1:5-7, NIV)

Dear friends, never take revenge. Leave that to the righteous anger of God. For the Scriptures say, "I will take revenge; I will pay them back," says the Lord. (Rom 12:19, NLT)

Prayer

Heavenly Father, in order that I may be and do today what you call me to be and do, strengthen me within. By your grace, may I be able to rule over my own spirit. Amen.

Other Spiritual Traits

We may take the nine virtues named in Galatians 5:22-23 as representative descriptions of the result of God's Holy Spirit at work in our lives. The next twenty-five devotions mention other biblical descriptions of how God works in us.

16 **Assurance**
Following the Good Shepherd

*The LORD is my shepherd; I shall not
want. He maketh me to lie down in
green pastures: he leadeth me beside
the still waters. He restoreth my soul:
he leadeth me in the paths of righteousness for his name's sake. Yea, though I
walk through the valley of the shadow
of death, I will fear no evil: for thou
art with me; thy rod and thy staff they
comfort me. Thou preparest a table
before me in the presence of mine
enemies: thou anointest my head with
oil; my cup runneth over. Surely goodness and mercy shall follow me all the
days of my life: and I will dwell in the
house of the LORD for ever. (Ps 23:1-6,
KJV)*

We sense perfect assurance in David's Twenty-third Psalm.
Sheep are supremely helpless animals: no horns, claws, fangs,
or stingers. They find their assurance in the shepherd: a strong
man, watchful and courageous, dedicated to his sheep.

Therefore we are assured, poised, at ease, confident.

The Good Shepherd (our God) leads us on good paths even
in the face of enemies, even in the face of death. He inspires
within us the sense that we are surrounded and followed all day
every day by God's goodness and mercy, and that our eternal
dwelling is with our shepherd.

A Quote to Remember

Assurance after all is no more than a full-grown faith; a . . . faith that grasps Christ's promise with both hands, a faith that argues like the good centurion, if the Lord "speak the word only," I am healed. Wherefore then should I doubt?[20] (J. C. Ryle)

Think on These Things

And the work of righteousness shall be peace; and the effect of righteousness quietness and assurance forever. And my people shall dwell in a peaceable habitation, and in sure dwellings, and in quiet resting places. (Isa 32:17-18, KJV)

I am the good shepherd; I know my sheep and my sheep know me, just as the Father knows me and I know the Father, and I lay down my life for the sheep. (John 10:11-15, NIV)

In all these things we are more than conquerors through him who loved us. For I am convinced that neither death nor life . . . will be able to separate us from the love of God that is in Christ Jesus our Lord. (Rom 8:37-39, NIV)

Prayer

Great Good Shepherd, I'm glad to recognize now my dependence on you and your supremely able care for me. Grant me increasing assurance, I pray, as I follow your leading and obey your commands. Amen.

17 **Compassion**
Making the Difference

*But a certain Samaritan, as he jour-
neyed, came where he was: and when
he saw him, he had compassion on
him. (Luke 10:33, KJV)*

See how important compassion is in God's eyes? Some of Jesus'
opponents asked him, "Who is my neighbor?" In answer, Jesus
told a parable about a man who was robbed, beaten, and left
for dead by the roadside. We might expect that the two religious leaders would stop to help, but they passed by. Then a
Samaritan, hated by Jews as a half-breed, stopped and helped
the wounded man. He "had compassion on him."

Jesus asked, "Who was neighbor to the wounded man?"

Think. Do we really see what Jesus did? He turned the tables
on his questioners. They had asked, "Who is my neighbor?"
Ignoring their query, Jesus forced them to answer another question: "Are you a neighborly person?"

What virtue made the difference between the one who
stopped to help and those who did not? Compassion! Compassion made the difference. It still does.

Those with religious credentials honored by people aren't
necessarily the most compassionate people in God's eyes. And
those who have none of those religious credentials may be
esteemed more highly in God's eyes. God's view and the world's
view often are backwards from each other, and the matter hinges
on compassion.

A Quote to Remember

Compassion is the ultimate and most meaningful embodiment of emotional maturity. It is through compassion that a person achieves the highest peak and deepest reach in his or her search for self-fulfillment.[21] (Arthur Jersild)

Think on These Things

As a father has compassion on his children, so the LORD has compassion on those who fear him. (Ps 103:13, NIV)

The LORD's lovingkindnesses indeed never cease, for His compassions never fail. They are new every morning; great is Your faithfulness. (Lam 3:22-23, NASB)

Therefore, as God's chosen people, holy and dearly loved, clothe yourselves with compassion, kindness, humility, gentleness and patience. (Col 3:12, NIV)

Prayer

Compassionate God, I praise you for your care for me and for so many other wounded and unworthy souls along life's highways. You have loved us, lifted us up from the side of the road, and placed our feet on the highway to heaven. I pray for the spiritual ability to practice compassion today, for those who deserve it and especially for those who don't. Grant me grace to see people through your eyes of compassion. Amen.

18 **Confidence**
Living with Calm, Quiet, Inward Security

Now as they observed the confidence of Peter and John and understood that they were uneducated and untrained men, they were amazed, and began to recognize them as having been with Jesus. (Acts 4:13, NASV)

The apostles had been arrested for preaching about Jesus. The pompous authorities expected them to be fearful, arrogant, or blustery. They were surprised to hear the disciple duo speak with calm dignity, respect, and self-assurance. It was an attitude, a level of self-esteem, a manner and bearing they had seen before. They had seen it in Jesus.

Christian confidence does not mean flying in the face of those who fly in our faces. Ferocious fighting back is often evidence of a lack of confidence: a fear that all could be lost if we do not out-argue someone. That ferocity is sometimes thought to be boldness and confidence, but it is not that at all. Confidence is an even-handedness when we get treated unjustly. It is unruffled speech rather than rude shouting. It is testifying and reasoning rather than accusing and arguing. It is poise and composure as opposed to frustration and exasperation.

Such confidence and self-esteem has effects in two directions. First, we are less likely to lose control. Second, others are reminded of the power of our Lord, just as the Sanhedrin members were amazed at Peter's and John's confidence.

Quotes to Remember

There is overwhelming evidence that the higher the level of self-esteem, the more likely one will be to treat others with respect, kindness, and generosity.[22] (Nathaniel Branden)

I was always looking outside myself for strength and confidence but it comes from within. It is there all the time.[23] (Anna Freud)

Think on These Things

For thus said the Lord GOD, the Holy One of Israel, "In returning and rest you shall be saved; in quietness and in trust shall be your strength." (Isa 30:15, ESV)

For the LORD will be your confidence and will keep your foot from being snared. (Prov 3:26, NIV)

Paul dwelt two whole years in his own hired house, and received all that came in unto him, preaching the kingdom of God, and teaching those things which concern the Lord Jesus Christ, with all confidence, no man forbidding him. (Acts 28:30-31, KJV)

Prayer

Heavenly Father, virtues are easier said than done, and confidence is no exception. I see it from afar, but I'm not there yet. Build me up on the inside, I pray, that today I may experience for myself and demonstrate to others the confidence that you still give to your disciples. Amen.

19 Discretion
Having Prudence, Tact, and Diplomacy

Daniel handled the situation with wisdom and discretion. (Dan 2:14, NLT)

Daniel and Nabal make a marvelously revealing comparison about the value of discretion. Nabal was "surly and mean" (1 Sam 25:3, NIV). On one occasion he insulted David needlessly, and David started on his way with armed men to teach Nabal a lesson. Fortunately, Nabal's wife persuaded David to overlook the rudeness of her husband, whom she called "a fool" (1 Sam 25:25).

Daniel and all the other wise men in the kingdom were to be put to death because no one could interpret King Nebuchadnezzar's dream. Daniel "handled the situation with wisdom and discretion" (Dan 2:4, NLT). Daniel's death sentence was revoked, and Nebuchadnezzar promoted Daniel and his three close friends to high positions of authority and respect.

Here's the telling comparison: Nabal was in no particular danger when his indiscretion almost got him killed. Daniel was under sentence of death when his discretion won him a huge promotion in the government.

In any situation, whether one of great danger or no danger at all, tact and diplomacy pay off. Prudence and good judgment are the way to go. Such discretion is not only right and godly; it's the only wise and sensible way to speak and act.

Quotes to Remember

A prudent silence will frequently be taken for wisdom and a sentence or two cautiously thrown in will sometimes gain the palm of knowledge, while a man well informed but indiscreet and unreserved will not uncommonly talk himself out of all consideration and weight.[24] (Alexander Hamilton)

Mutual respect implies discretion and reserve even in love itself; it means preserving as much liberty as possible to those whose life we share.[25] (Henri Frederic Amiel)

Nothing is more dangerous than a friend without discretion; even a prudent enemy is preferable.[26] (Jean de La Fontaine)

Think on These Things

My son, do not let wisdom and understanding out of your sight, preserve sound judgment and discretion. (Prov 3:21, NIV)

I, wisdom, dwell together with prudence; I possess knowledge and discretion. (Prov 8:12, NIV)

Discretion is a life-giving fountain to those who possess it. (Prov 16:22, NLT)

Prayer

God, thank you for being the source of all prudence and discretion for those who seek your face. Grant to me good judgment and tact in all my conversations today. Enable me by your grace to exercise restraint and disciplined speech and actions, especially when neglecting them would bring harm to me and sorrow to you. In all I do and say today and every day, grant me discretion that my life may honor you. In Jesus' name. Amen.

20 Encouragement
Being a Stepping-stone

So encourage each other and build each other up, just as you are already doing. (1 Thess 5:11, NLT)

Religion is relational; it has to do with how we relate to others. Every interaction by word or deed helps or harms. We place in others' paths either a hurdle or a stepping-stone. We are either headwinds holding them back or tailwinds moving them forward.

The Bible speaks often of encouragement, sometimes translated as "comfort." God instructed Moses to encourage his successor Joshua (Deut 3:28); we are to encourage the disheartened (1 Thess 5:14); we should encourage one another (1 Thess 4:18); Paul sent Tychicus to the Ephesians to encourage them (Eph 6:21-22); and Paul prayed for God to encourage the Thessalonians (2 Thess 2:17).

We recall people who have encouraged us, especially those who were thoughtful when others were not, who spoke an uplifting word in a difficult time. Such recollections should prompt us to look for opportunities to encourage someone else who is suffering. May we establish the habit of encouragement. That's how we should relate to one another.

A Quote to Remember

Isn't it strange, that princes and kings,
and clowns that caper in sawdust rings,
And common folk like you and me
are the builders of eternity?
To each is given a bag of tools,

a shapeless mass and a book of rules;
and each must make, ere time is flown,
a stumbling-block or a stepping-stone.[27] (R. L. Sharpe)

Think on These Things

And we urge you, brothers and sisters, warn those who are idle
and disruptive, encourage the disheartened, help the weak, be
patient with everyone. (1 Thess 5:14, NIV)

May our Lord Jesus Christ himself and God our Father, who
loved us and by his grace gave us eternal encouragement and
good hope, encourage your hearts and strengthen you in every
good deed and word. (2 Thess 2:16, NIV)

I long to see you so that I may impart to you some spiritual gift
to make you strong—that is, that you and I may be mutually
encouraged by each other's faith. (Rom 1:11-12, NIV)

Prayer

God of encouragement, I worship you as the one who lifts my
spirit and causes me to be glad, even in the midst of pain and
suffering. Guide my steps in paths of encouragement: to the
handicapped in body or in spirit, to the lonely, to the secretly
discouraged. Help me get my thoughts and priorities off myself,
and train my words and actions for the benefit of those who
need your encouragement through me. Amen.

21 Forgiving Heart
Allowing an Endless Second Chance

Forgive us our sins, as we have forgiven those who sin against us.
(Matt 6:12, NLT)

Then Peter came to him and asked, "Lord, how often should I forgive someone who sins against me? Seven times?" "No, not seven times," Jesus replied, "but seventy times seven!"
(Matt 18:21-22, NIV)

These two passages reveal the nature of forgiveness as God sees it. The first verse is part of the prayer that the Lord taught us to pray. Like the rest of that prayer, it's something of a challenge. Do we really want God to forgive us the same way we have forgiven those who have sinned against us? There is a powerful if subtle point: our forgiving hearts, or our lack of forgiving hearts, determines whether we are able to receive God's forgiveness. One who forgives is able to receive forgiveness; one who does not forgive cannot be forgiven.

The second passage reinforces the same truth. When Jesus said "seventy times seven," what he meant was "Peter, stop counting. Be a forgiving person. Have a forgiving heart." If we're counting how many times we forgive someone, waiting for the magic number when we are justified in being harsh, judgmental, and unforgiving, we'll never get there. There is no such number. Forgiveness is not about counting; it's about having a forgiving spirit and a heart that wants to forgive. It's about offering endless second chances to others the way God does to us.

A Quote to Remember

He that cannot forgive others, breaks the bridge over which he himself must pass if he would ever reach heaven; for everyone has need to be forgiven.[28] (George Herbert)

Think on These Things

For thou, Lord, art good, and ready to forgive; and plenteous in mercy unto all them that call upon thee. (Ps 86:5, KJV)

And when you stand praying, if you hold anything against anyone, forgive them, so that your Father in heaven may forgive you your sins. (Mark 11:25, NIV)

Pay attention to yourselves! If your brother sins, rebuke him, and if he repents, forgive him, and if he sins against you seven times in the day, and turns to you seven times, saying, "I repent," you must forgive him. (Luke 17:3-4, ESV)

Prayer

Forgiving Lord, I confess that I've been counting too much to excuse grudges and ill feelings. Set me free, I pray. May a forgiving spirit replace the arithmetic I've used to ask you to be more forgiving toward me than I have been toward those whom I consider sinners against me. Amen.

22 **Gracious Speech**
Harnessing the Gift of Words

Let your conversation be gracious and attractive so that you will have the right response for everyone. (Col 4:6, NLT)

Gracious speech is easier to recognize than to define. We don't know how to explain it, but some of our friends seem to speak appropriately in every occasion, while others seem to speak in an abrasive and awkward tone.

The context of the verse above discusses how the people of God are to respond to those outside the faith: how to answer their questions and what points to make in the conversation. In that context, we certainly need to give attention to appropriate and gracious speech.

Moreover, gracious speech is to be desired in any and every conversation with loved ones, friends, mere acquaintances, and even enemies. Who has not regretted insinuating something unintended, or realizing too late that we said something in a way that insulted when we did not mean to be insulting? Like an infant who discovers for the first time the joy of throwing things, we too often throw our words without thought, care, or control of what they hit or whom they hurt.

Gracious speech improves with practice. Education plays a role. Command of language plays a role. But nothing accomplishes quite as much as a sincere resolve to develop the habit and the ability to speak with grace.

A Quote to Remember

A careless word may kindle strife;
A cruel word may wreck a life.

A bitter word may hate instill;
A brutal word may smite and kill.
A gracious word may smooth the way;
A joyous word may light the day.
A timely word may lessen stress;
A loving word may heal and bless.[29] (Author unknown)

Think on These Things

The wise in heart are called discerning, and gracious words promote instruction. (Prov 16:21, NIV)

Gracious words are a honeycomb, sweet to the soul and healing to the bones. (Prov 16:24, NIV)

One who loves a pure heart and who speaks with grace will have the king for a friend. (Prov 22:11, NIV)

Prayer

Lord, you know better than I that I've said some thoughtless and ungracious words. Please guard my heart and my words today, that I may speak with grace. Amen.

23 **Grief**
Finding Sources of Strength for Healthy Mourning

Yea, though I walk through the valley of the shadow of death, I will fear no evil: for thou art with me; thy rod and thy staff they comfort me. (Ps 23:4 KJV)

Grief at the death of a loved one can be managed in healthy and realistic ways, or it can be mismanaged in ways that debilitate us longer. There are sources of strength and comfort available to us. Christians find great comfort in the presence of our Good Shepherd, the Lord. Grief has much less power over those who fear no evil in death.

The Bible has dozens of passages that speak directly to our grief. Scripture also has a track record of encouraging those who read and meditate on it frequently.

It's important to select good memories and be intentional about focusing on them. We do not intend to deny the reality of other memories, but the healthy approach in looking back is to choose and dwell on thoughts that encourage and uplift us.

Gratitude is wonderful medicine. As we thank God for his blessings, the thankful attitude becomes a source of strength and stamina both emotionally and spiritually.

Give in to sadness and tears once in a while. Grief returns from time to time for months or even years. This is normal. Choose times and places to let loose, cry, remember, and be sad.

Be realistic. Refuse the naïve idea that at some point life will "return to normal." The healthy approach is to recognize that the passing of loved ones changes our lives so that we cannot go back to the way things were. We can, however, adjust and move on. Let's reflect on the thought that our deceased loved ones would want us to do that.

A Quote to Remember

Life is eternal, and love is immortal, and death is only a horizon; and a horizon is nothing save the limit of our sight.[30] (Rossiter Worthington Raymond)

Think on These Things

So the sons of Israel wept for Moses in the plains of Moab thirty days; then the days of weeping and mourning for Moses came to an end. (Deut 34:8, NASB)

So do not fear, for I am with you; do not be dismayed, for I am your God. I will strengthen you and help you; I will uphold you with my righteous right hand. (Isa 41:10, NIV)

Yet what we suffer now is nothing compared to the glory he will reveal to us later. (Rom 8:18, NLT)

Prayer

Lord of life and death, we pray for strength in these days of grieving. The tide of mixed emotions ebbs and flows, and we need the sense that our present dismay will give way to spiritual strength as we meditate on the Eternal God who is our dwelling place, and whose everlasting arms are underneath us (see Deut 33:27, NASB). Amen.

24 **Honesty**
Believing There Are No Ifs, Ands, or Buts

The LORD demands accurate scales
and balances; he sets the standards
for fairness. (Prov 16:11, NLT)

This verse is about a merchant weighing out a customer's goods. When the customer pays for a gallon or for a pound, the Lord demands a gallon delivered, or a pound, and not a drop or a hair less. Don't even begin to walk down a dishonest path.

But the command is about much more than buying and selling; it's about honesty and truthfulness. Other verses call for truthfulness in speech (Prov 12:22), in giving testimony in court (Exod 20:16), and in treating everyone the same (Deut 16:19-20).

The religious authorities of Jesus' day had some confusing guidelines about truthfulness. A person might explain an incident and then swear that it was the truth. If they swore by God's name, then they were bound to tell the truth. But if they swore by their mother, or by their life, and did not mention the name of God, then they were free not to tell the truth.

Jesus said that's ridiculous. A godly person's character should make swearing unnecessary. If a person says it's true, God expects it to be true—no ifs, ands, or buts (Matt 5:37).

Honesty is not about how to evade our responsibility to tell the truth. It's about the character and integrity that the Lord expects of us in everything we say and do.

A Quote to Remember

We tell lies when we are afraid . . . afraid of what we don't know, afraid of what others will think, afraid of what will be found out about us. But every time we tell a lie, the thing that we fear grows stronger.[31] (Tad Williams)

Think on These Things

The one who has clean hands and a pure heart, who does not trust in an idol or swear by a false god. They will receive blessing from the LORD. (Ps 24:4-5, NIV)

We have regard for what is honorable, not only in the sight of the LORD, but also in the sight of men. (2 Cor 8:21, NASB)

Don't lie to each other, for you have stripped off your old sinful nature and all its wicked deeds. (Col 3:9, NLT)

Prayer

God of truth, we praise you as the one who speaks honesty and declares what is right (Isa 45:19). Thank you for your Holy Spirit, who leads us into all truth. Thank you for your Son, who is full of grace and truth. Thank you that you are our ultimate standard of honesty. We desire to live honestly today, and to speak truth, not for ourselves alone but for the sake of a world in which untruth has a thousand faces and an unknown number of willing adherents. Make us, we pray, the salt of honesty and the light of truthfulness. Amen.

25 Hope
Looking Ahead with Expectation

Then, just as the LORD had said, my cousin Hanamel came to me in the courtyard of the guard and said, "Buy my field at Anathoth in the territory of Benjamin. Since it is your right to redeem it and possess it, buy it for yourself." I knew that this was the word of the LORD; so I bought the field at Anathoth. (Jer 32:8-9a, NIV)

Jeremiah was a master illustrator. In preaching he spoke about cucumbers, rotten figs, an ox yoke, a burning scroll, and much more. He also could act out his message, which he did memorably on the subject of hope.

At Jerusalem's darkest hour, just before its defeat by Babylon, the city was surrounded. Having gained almost everyone's disfavor, Jeremiah was little more than a prisoner himself when the Lord directed him to live out a parable of hope. *Let me show you what hope looks like,* God must have thought. Hopelessness was rampant; everyone realized that the king could not resist the mighty Babylonians. Soon, all property would belong to the enemy. Even so, the Lord instructed Jeremiah to buy property near his hometown, Anathoth. Such a purchase would demonstrate faith and hope for the future (Jer 32:6-15).

Prophets always are a step or two ahead of the rest of us. When the people could not see judgment and destruction ahead, Jeremiah did. When they could not see hope beyond the judgment, Jeremiah did.

Sometimes we too struggle to keep hope alive. And just as Jeremiah counseled his peers to hope in God, we may find hope in that same divine source. In our darkest hours, and in all hours, God is the one who sees tomorrow and instills hope today.

A Quote to Remember

Hope is the thing with feathers
That perches in the soul
And sings the tune without the words
And never stops at all.[32] (Emily Dickinson)

Think on These Things

Know that wisdom is thus [like honey] for your soul. If you find it, then there will be a future, and your hope will not be cut off. (Prov 24:14, NASB)

If we have hoped in Christ in this life only, we are of all men most to be pitied. (1 Cor 15:19, NASB)

Such things were written in the Scriptures long ago to teach us. And the Scriptures give us hope and encouragement as we wait patiently for God's promises to be fulfilled. (Rom 15:4, NLT)

Prayer

Heavenly Father, we are your humble servants, coming to you today in need of hope. At times we feel weak and helpless. We pray for a better future, a better life. Help us to find hope in you. Amen.

26 **Hopeful**
Holding Fast to Hope

Let us hold tightly without wavering
to the hope we affirm, for God can
be trusted to keep his promise.
(Heb 10:23, NLT)

The tenth chapter of Hebrews mentions reasons for us to hope in the Lord: Christ's sacrifice for the forgiveness of our sins, God's covenant with us, and our confidence in drawing near to God. Hope is an evergreen, perennial virtue to all who strive for it.

Therefore let us "grasp firmly" (Heb 12:23, ABPE) or "hold unwaveringly" (Heb 10:23, NET) to our hope in the Lord. We can trust God to keep his promises. We can choose to live all day, every day, in every situation, with this positive and hopeful outlook. It pervades our nature. It colors, shapes, and dominates every life experience, even death itself.

We're told that in the darkness of deep space, a light as tiny as a candle could be seen thousands of miles away. That's because the darkness accentuates the light. In the worst of circumstances, when we are engulfed in the darkness of deep hopelessness, that darkness actually accentuates the light of hope. For our own sakes, for the sake of others who have no hope, and for the sake of the gospel, hold tightly to Christian hope.

Quotes to Remember

Hope begins in the dark, the stubborn hope that if you just show up and try to do the right thing, the dawn will come.[33] (Anne Lamott)

When you say a situation or a person is hopeless, you're slamming the door in the face of God.[34] (Charles L. Allen)

Think on These Things

So we fix our eyes not on what is seen, but on what is unseen, since what is seen is temporary, but what is unseen is eternal. (2 Cor 4:18, NIV)

Be of good courage, and he shall strengthen your heart, all ye that hope in the LORD. (Ps 31:24, KJV)

Yet those who wait for the LORD will gain new strength; They will mount up with wings like eagles, They will run and not get tired, They will walk and not become weary. For I know the plans I have for you, says the LORD. They are plans for good and not for disaster, to give you a future and a hope. (Isa 40:31, NASB; Jer 29:11, NLT)

Prayer

God of hope, I come to you now as an humble servant much in need of hope. Events and the realities of life have distorted my thinking, and I feel weak and helpless. I pray for hope. Tune my heart to receive your love and comfort. Transform my spirit to take joy once again in the faith that, while I am not in control, you are. O Lord, touch me now with hope, I pray. Amen.

27 **Justice**
Defending the Oppressed

Defend the poor and fatherless; do
justice to the afflicted and needy.
Deliver the poor and needy; free
them from the hand of the wicked.
(Ps 82:3-4, NKJV)

Justice in the Old Testament was primarily about treating the poor and oppressed with kindness and fairness. The need for it arose under social customs and laws that made it acceptable for some to be wealthy while others were trapped in poverty. Justice is closely related to compassion expressed in social and economic customs.

One character quality that remains strong among the Lord's people is justice. It's not difficult to find CEOs with seven-digit salaries plus perks. The perks alone often amount to more than the annual income of some of the oppressed who help pay for those absurd salaries.

When friends and relatives perpetuate these wrongs, our looking the other way and saying nothing keeps us imprisoned behind the bars of injustice. Peace of mind and a heart for individuals and for nations lie beyond overcoming unjust ways. The sense of assurance and security that everyone longs for can come only from a God who commands us to do justice for the afflicted and the needy.

A Quote to Remember

A true revolution of values will soon cause us to question the fairness and justice of many of our past and present policies. On the one hand we are called to play the Good Samaritan on life's roadside, but that will be only an initial act. One day we must come to see that the whole Jericho Road must be transformed so that men and women will not be constantly beaten and robbed as they make their journey on life's highway. True compassion is more than flinging a coin to a beggar. It comes to see that an edifice which produces beggars needs restructuring.[35] (Martin Luther King, Jr.)

Think on These Things

If you see a poor person being oppressed by the powerful and justice being miscarried throughout the land, don't be surprised! For every official is under orders from higher up, and matters of justice only get lost in red tape and bureaucracy. (Eccl 5:8, NLT)

Learn to do good. Seek justice. Help the oppressed. Defend the cause of orphans. Fight for the rights of widows. (Isa 1:17, NLT)

I want to see a mighty flood of justice, an endless river of righteous living. (Amos 5:24, NLT)

Prayer

God of justice, forgive my failure to do what I can to bring about justice in my little corner of the world. Continue calling my conscience to speak up for all who suffer injustice and economic oppression in our society. In Jesus' name, amen.

28 Legacy
Establishing a Good Name

A good name is more desirable than great riches; to be esteemed is better than silver or gold. (Prov 22:1, NIV)

I knocked on the timid lady's door. I was a junior in high school, selling magazines. After a long time the door finally cracked open a little. I could see one eye as she peeped out and said, "Who is it?" As I started to introduce myself and my task, suddenly the door flew wide open. "Oh, you're Bob Frazier's boy, aren't you? Come on in!" She bought three subscriptions.

I thought I must be a pretty good salesman, because all over the community I sold magazines. At some point I realized that it was my dad, not me, who was the salesman. I earned a nice wristwatch selling magazines, but actually my father earned it. He's long gone, but the inheritance he left me, the good name, still follows me around. I go by the cemetery from time to time and thank him and Mama for my roots.

As blessed as I am to have inherited a good name, it is better still to create a good name for those who follow us. Dwelling on legacies we have received, however, is self-centered; it's better to focus on legacies we leave for others.

Also, we often leave a godly legacy to someone other than those in our biological families. Many dedicated Christians have had the tremendously edifying experience of hearing something like this: "You probably were not aware of what a great influence you had on me years ago, but you did. Thank you."

That's a good legacy. That's leaving a good name.

Quotes to Remember

Regard your good name as the richest jewel you can possibly be possessed of. For credit is like fire; when once you have kindled it you may easily preserve it, but if you once extinguish it, you will find it an arduous task to rekindle it again. The way to gain a good reputation is to endeavor to be what you desire to appear.[36] (Socrates)

The legacy of heroes is the memory of a great name and the inheritance of a great example.[37] (Benjamin Disraeli)

Think on These Things

My son, do not forget my teaching, but keep my commands in your heart, for they will prolong your life many years and bring you peace and prosperity. Let love and faithfulness never leave you; bind them around your neck, write them on the tablet of your heart. Then you will win favor and a good name in the sight of God and man. (Prov 3:1-4, NIV)

The memory of the righteous is a blessing, but the name of the wicked will rot. Choose a good reputation over great riches; being held in high esteem is better than silver or gold. (Prov 10:7, ESV; 22:1, NLT)

. . . Cornelius the centurion. He is a righteous and God-fearing man, who is respected by all the Jewish people. (Acts 10:22, NIV)

Prayer

God, thank you for those whose good names bear me up and keep me true today. Help me to build that kind of legacy and good name for others. Amen.

29 Loneliness
When No One Comes to Visit

*As for my friends and my neighbors,
they stand aloof from my distress; even
my close relatives stand at a distance.
(Ps 38:11, ISV)*

Different sources suggest different remedies for loneliness: meditating, socializing, active solitude, shopping. What not to do seems clear: don't give in to sadness and self-pity. There are other ways to feel less lonely.

Cultivate friendship with the Lord. Just as daily exercise and keeping fit help us remain stronger through stress, surgery recovery, or hard physical labor, daily meditation over time helps us remain stronger emotionally through loneliness. When we have walked and talked with the Lord daily for years, we have an instinctive, intrinsic sense that we are not alone because he is with us. Today is the best day to begin or to strengthen daily meditation.

Work in solitude. Do something. Do anything. Read, walk, write, play music. Being alone is not the same as being lonely. We can be lonely even in a crowd of people. The key is to make our time alone productive.

Spend some money. Shopping gets us out into the hustle and bustle of life. Those who can't get out physically can shop through magazines, catalogues, or the Internet; it's still a way to get our minds somewhere else. Getting into the activity of the world around us can help us feel less alone.

Interact with someone else. Call a friend. Write a friend. Go to see a friend. Once a day, initiate a genial interaction with someone. Make a mental note of what that person is concerned about today, and remember to ask about that concern tomorrow.

When you walk a long and lonely road, look upward. Unchallenged loneliness spreads in concentric waves. It may not be easy to conquer loneliness, but by God's grace it is possible.

A Quote to Remember

City life is millions of people being lonesome together.[38] (Henry David Thoreau)

Think on These Things

He reached down from heaven and rescued me; he drew me out of deep waters. (2 Sam 22:17, NLT)

He also brought me forth into a broad place; He rescued me, because He delighted in me. (2 Sam 22:20, NIV)

I sought the LORD, and he answered me; he delivered me from all my fears. (Ps 34:4, NIV)

Prayer

Lord Jesus, you have faced the loneliness we face. Enable us to overcome as you did. Our minds get flooded with several different kinds of thoughts and feelings that can drown a person mentally. Draw us out of these deep waters, we pray. Amen.

30 **Patriotism**
Demonstrating the Spirit of Christian Citizenship

Give to Caesar what belongs to him.
(Matt 22:21)

What belongs to Caesar? What do we owe government officials? In this section of devotions, we are reflecting on Christian spirits or attitudes. Many people think instinctively that any serious sharing of ideas has to be combative, maneuvering and manipulating others in conversation. But God's children can provide examples of a better way. The Bible tells us what we owe our government officials. Let's take note of these four debts and then talk politics within those parameters.

First, we owe government officials our prayers. "Pray this way for kings and all who are in authority so that we can live peaceful and quiet lives marked by godliness and dignity" (1 Tim 2:2, NLT).

Second, we owe obedience. "Let everyone be subject to the governing authorities, for there is no authority except that which God has established. The authorities that exist have been established by God" (Rom 13:1, NIV).

Third, we owe financial support. "This is also why you pay taxes, for the authorities are God's servants" (Rom 13:6, NIV).

Fourth, we owe them respect. "Give to everyone what you owe them: if you owe taxes, pay taxes; if revenue, then revenue; if respect, then respect; if honor, then honor" (Rom 13:7, NIV).

The point is not whether officials deserve our respect. The point is that the office of government deserves it. If that's not enough, then God commands it, and isn't that enough? For we are to do everything "as to the Lord" (Col 3:23, KJV).

A Quote to Remember

We must learn to live together as brothers, or we will perish together as fools.[39] (Martin Luther King Jr.)

Think on These Things

You are the salt of the earth. You are the light of the world. (Matt 5:13-14, NIV)

I tell you that every careless word that people speak, they shall give an accounting for it in the day of judgment. (Matt 12:36, NASB)

If you bite and devour one another, take care that you are not consumed by one another. (Gal 5:15, NASB)

Prayer

Almighty God, you have given us a good land as our heritage. Forgive us for badmouthing those who lead. Make us mindful, we pray, of the debts that you place upon us regarding our public servants. Help us meet our debts to you and to them, thereby helping them carry out their responsibilities. Concerning our speech and actions about citizenship, prompt us to do everything as if we do it to you. Amen.

31 A Quiet Life
Living at Peace with One's Self

Make it your goal to live a quiet life, minding your own business and working with your hands, just as we instructed you before. (1 Thess 4:11, NLT)

One great embarrassment of Christians is that we talk so much and so loudly. Interviews and conversations of all kinds often remind us of a pride of lions feeding, snapping and snarling, each lunging in for a moment and then getting shoved aside by others.

The rudeness of too much talk, quick-draw responses without reflection, and the obsession with speaking to every issue and answering every question are bruising and tiring to others. The courteous individual is by and large a quiet person, unfazed by others' frantic conversation. The quiet life does not seek the spotlight, and may actually be embarrassed by it.

And in truth, the quietness Paul mentions in his letter to the Thessalonians is about much more than words. It's about a spirit, a healthy attitude toward one's self, others, and life. A quiet life testifies to being at peace with one's self, while incessant talking and scurrying about testify to an emptiness and the frantic search to fill it.

Jesus certainly could hold his own with those who attacked him verbally and maliciously. But the New Testament paints numerous pictures of him as a quiet man: peacefully asleep in a boat during a storm (Luke 8:23), kneeling without a word and writing in the sand while angry people prepared to stone a lady caught in adultery (John 8:6), and making "still no reply" to

Pilate for all the false and hypocritical charges brought against him (Mark 15:5, NIV). He delivered his most famous speech, the Sermon on the Mount, on a quiet mountainside (Matt 5–7). Sometimes after doing some front-page type of miracle, he sternly told his disciples not to speak of it to anyone (Matt 9:30).

A Quote to Remember

Quiet minds cannot be perplexed or frightened, but go on in fortune or in misfortune at their own private pace, like a clock during a thunderstorm.[40] (Robert Louis Stevenson)

Think on These Things

Don't sin by letting anger control you. Think about it overnight and remain silent. (Ps 4:4, NLT)

Be still, and know that I am God! In quietness and trust is your strength. (Ps 46:10, NLT; Isa 30:15, NIV)

Let your adorning be the hidden person of the heart with the imperishable beauty of a gentle and quiet spirit, which in God's sight is very precious. (1 Pet 3:4, ESV)

Prayer

Lord of the stillness, call forth in my heart the peace and purpose that shows itself in a gentle and quiet life. Help me find peace within, no matter what is going on around me. Amen.

32 **Reverence**
Showing Awe, Respect, and Honor

Fear the LORD, you his godly people,
for those who fear him will have all they
need. (Ps 34:9, NLT)

We fear disappointing our loved ones; we fear that we'll hurt someone's feelings. This is the kind of fear the Bible most often means when it says "fear the Lord." There is indeed an element of being afraid of God, but the focus is on awe, respect, and honor.

The word "hallow" or "hallowed" carries the same meaning: to revere the name of God. When Jesus taught us to pray, "Hallowed be thy name" (Luke 11:2, KJV), he meant that we should be thoughtful and respectful in using God's name. We should not speak the name of God carelessly, because we will be judged for every careless word we speak (Matt 12:36, ESV). Surely that holds doubly true for the way we speak God's name.

We recognize two kinds of irreverence, one through familiarity and the other through outright disrespect and dishonor. Familiarity with religious language and the Scriptures can pose a quiet, creeping danger for those of us who have spent a lot of time reading the Bible and worshiping in church. We hear and talk so much about religious things that we cease to show due reverence for the Lord, the church, and the Bible.

The other kind of irreverence is the outright disrespect that we perceive in Pharaoh's retort to Moses: "Who is the LORD that I should obey him?" (Exod 5:2, NIV). He was sarcastic, cutting, disrespectful, irreverent. Perhaps we know individuals who treat God this way.

Be a reverent person.

A Quote to Remember

Gratitude bestows reverence, allowing us to encounter everyday epiphanies, those transcendent moments of awe that change forever how we experience life and the world.[41] (John Milton)

Think on These Things

Reverence for the LORD is the foundation of true wisdom. (Ps 111:9-10, NLT)

God, the blessed and only Ruler, the King of kings and Lord of lords, who alone is immortal and who lives in unapproachable light, whom no one has seen or can see. To him be honor and might forever. Amen. (1 Tim 6:15-16, NIV)

Let us be thankful and please God by worshiping him with holy fear and awe. (Heb 12:28, NLT)

Prayer

Our Father, who art in heaven, hallowed be thy name. I resolve now to revere you today, to respect your name, to honor you by all I do and say. Still, I am afraid that through carelessness I will disappoint you. Make me alert every moment to revere you. Amen.

33 **Spirituality**
Being Filled with the Spirit

Be filled with the Spirit. (Eph 5:18, KJV)

One biblical, practical, and understandable explanation of being filled with God's Spirit is having an abundance of the nine virtues named in Galatians 5:22-23: love, joy, peace, patience, kindness, goodness, faithfulness, gentleness, and self-control. These virtues describe the fruit, or the results, of God's presence at work in us. We may say that these traits are what spirituality is.

There are other legitimate biblical explanations of spirituality, or being filled with the spirit. However, someone who gives no evidence of the spirits and attitudes described in Galatians 5:22-23 can make no credible claim to being spirit filled, regardless of which biblical explanation they prefer. We can work in the church without being spiritual. We can tithe or give to the poor and still not be spiritual. These nine virtues and others similar to them in the New Testament (such as reverence, forgiveness, confidence, and encouragement) are the proof of identity for any who claim to be spirit filled.

This approach to spirituality gives us something specific and understandable to work toward: we are cultivating love in our interactions with others; we look for reasons to be joyful; we function as peacemakers. This approach also enables us to assess how and where we fail. Finally, it provides a basis for choosing our friends: we choose those who exemplify these godly traits. May the spirituality perspective invade our minds and take over our lives.

A Quote to Remember

Just as in the previous verses Paul set out the evil things which are characteristic of the flesh, so now he sets out the lovely things which are the fruit of the Spirit.... It was Paul's belief and experience that the Christian died with Christ and rose again to a life, new and clean, in which the evil things of the old self are gone and the lovely things of the Spirit have come to fruition.[42] (William Barclay)

Think on These Things

And everyone present was filled with the Holy Spirit and began speaking in other languages, as the Holy Spirit gave them this ability. (Acts 2:4, NLT)

Do you not know that you are a temple of God and that the Spirit of God dwells in you? (1 Cor 3:16, NASB)

So I say, let the Holy Spirit guide your lives. Then you won't be doing what your sinful nature craves. (Gal 5:16, NLT)

Prayer

Heavenly Father, baptize me in your Spirit, I pray. Fill me to overflowing with those traits that identify your children and demonstrate your grace and wisdom to a world desperately in need of you. By your life in me, may I be Spirit-filled today. Amen.

34 Being Submissive
Seeking Humility out of Reverence for Christ

Submit to one another out of reverence for Christ. (Eph 5:21, NIV)

All of you be subject one to another. (1 Pet 5:5, KJV)

Christian submission is an attitude, a spirit. It is Christlike humility and modesty. It is a quality for the boss toward the employee as well as for the employee toward the boss. It is for the law enforcement officer toward the citizen and vice versa. Christian submission is for all of us, toward every person. It grows out of our reverence for Christ.

We may understand it better by thinking of the formula that Jesus used six times in his Sermon on the Mount: "you have heard it said . . . but I say to you" (Matt 5:17-48). If we apply that formula to Christian submission it might read, "you have heard it said that submission is about who has authority over whom, but I say to you that submission is about a Christlike spirit and an attitude of humility that all of you have toward everyone."

What does this mean for us? Our cue is the way Jesus treated people whom others treated disrespectfully. He was humble and modest toward all: tax collectors, prostitutes, lepers, beggars, and even his enemies. He saw himself as a servant.

In matters of submission, no line of authority is right enough. We must stop devising schemes about who can lord it over whom and start being humble and submissive people.

Christian submissiveness is a matter of the spirit, the heart, and our attitudes toward one another based on our attitude toward Christ.

A Quote to Remember

Submission is not about authority and it is not obedience; it is all about relationships of love and respect.[43] (William Paul Young)

Think on These Things

Who is more important, the one who sits at the table or the one who serves? The one who sits at the table, of course. But not here! For I am among you as one who serves. (Luke 22:27, NLT)

After that, he poured water into a basin and began to wash his disciples' feet, drying them with the towel that was wrapped around him. (John 13:5, NIV)

He [Jesus] gave up his divine privileges; he took the humble position of a slave and was born as a human being. (Phil 2:7, NLT)

Prayer

God, I praise you for Jesus, who made himself submissive to the whims of people who were ungodly to the point of crucifying him. I confess my predisposition not to submit to anybody. I submit even to you, O God, only when you act according to my pronouncements about how you act. Forgive me, I pray, and teach my heart submissiveness. Amen.

35 **Strength**
Demonstrating Strength in the Lord

Be strong in the Lord and in his mighty power. (Eph 6:10, NIV)

What kind of strength identifies a child of God, a follower of Christ? That's an important consideration. A low score is good in golf but a high score is good in basketball, so it's important to know what kind of score, and what kind of strength, we have in mind.

What does it mean to "be strong in the Lord"? Be strong in faith that perseveres in difficulty. Be strong in love that does not give in to hatred. Be strong in peacemaking; don't get drawn into combativeness. Be strong in kindness; don't respond to rudeness with rudeness. We want Christ's characteristics to be strong in us. He's the one we want most to please.

Focus on spiritual strengths rather than physical, worldly, or economic strength. It's okay to be wealthy if our primary strength is spiritual. There's nothing wrong with being a champion weightlifter in our age class unless we're wimps in the Christlike virtues.

Of course, no one can become strong simply by deciding to be strong. But it's also true that no one is strong without wanting to be strong. The first step is the right desire: dissatisfaction with fear and weakness along with the resolution and commitment to be strong in spiritual kinds of strength—strong in the Lord.

A Quote to Remember

People have always had God's help. Joseph was sold into Egypt, but the Lord was with Joseph. The Hebrew children were thrown into the furnace of fire, but there was a fourth Person in the flames, and his countenance was like that of the Son of God. The disciples were in the midst of the storm, but the Master of the storm came to them. The two on the road to Emmaus were joined by a Third, and the disciples' hearts were warmed as that Third opened the Scriptures to them. Stephen was stoned, but he was aware of the Christ; Paul experienced the loss of all his friends, but he testified, "The Lord stood by me." John was exiled to Patmos, but he "was in the Spirit on the Lord's day" (Rev 1:10, NASB). We get help.[44] (J. Winston Pearce)

Think on These Things

Have I not commanded you? Be strong and courageous. Do not be afraid; do not be discouraged, for the LORD your God will be with you wherever you go. (Josh 1:9, NIV)

For God has not given us a spirit of fear and timidity, but of power, love, and self-discipline. (2 Tim 1:7, NLT)

I can do everything through Christ, who gives me strength. (Phil 4:13, NLT)

Prayer

Almighty God, source of all strength, empower me within, I pray, not that I will be lifted out of the difficulties before me but that I will be strong in your mighty power. Amen.

36 **Thankfulness**
Giving Thanks Always

Give thanks in all circumstances; for this is God's will for you in Christ Jesus. (1 Thess 5:18, NIV)

Vitamins, exercise, low-fat diet, lots of water. How much attention and priority do we give to good health? However much the mind affects our health, that's how much a perennially thankful attitude boosts good health.

Thankfulness is healing. Positive and appreciative people heal from minor cuts and major surgeries better than habitual gripers.

Thankfulness is therapeutic, like sunlight that cheers the soul and makes life's pathways delightful.

Thankfulness is like a tailwind that makes forward movement easier; it's like a spring breeze that brings hope.

We must be careful to understand what the Bible actually says about giving thanks in trouble. God does not expect us to give thanks that we had a permanently debilitating accident, or that a friend is dying in terrible suffering day after day.

The understanding more likely to boost our spiritual health is that we are not necessarily to give thanks *for* everything but to give thanks *in* everything. God commands that we look for something to be thankful about. Some days we have more reasons to give thanks, some days fewer reasons. But every day of our lives, even when we're enveloped in catastrophe, it's a spiritually healthy habit to identify the reasons to give thanks, to think about them, to focus on them.

A Quote to Remember

Thanksgiving is an outlook; it's a good habit year round. (author unknown)

Think on These Things

They were also to stand every morning to thank and praise the LORD. They were to do the same in the evening. (1 Chron 23:30, NIV)

Then we your people, the sheep of your pasture, will thank you forever and ever, praising your greatness from generation to generation. (Ps 79:13, NLT)

Through Him then, let us continually offer up a sacrifice of praise to God, that is, the fruit of lips that give thanks to His name. (Heb 13:15, NASB)

Prayer

Lord of all good blessings, we praise you that you have given us so much to be thankful for. Plant and cultivate in us the habit of expressing to you constantly our gratitude that we have these bright spots, these good and perfect gifts from you day after day. Grant us the ability to conquer the negative stuff by reflecting on the positive stuff. Thank you, Lord. Amen.

37 Thoughts
Controlling the Mind

Fix your thoughts on what is true, and honorable, and right, and pure, and lovely, and admirable. Think about things that are excellent and worthy of praise. (Phil 4:8, NLT)

On our worst day, we can think of something to be glad about. On our best day, we can think of something to be sad about. Each of us is prone to let our thoughts wander like a ship without a rudder, according to our moods and the circumstances of the day. The Bible recognizes the wisdom of choosing our thoughts, of disciplining our minds.

Someone has said that we cannot prevent the birds of bad thoughts from passing overhead, but we can keep them from nesting in our hair or in our minds. So we "fix our thoughts," as Paul wrote to the Philippians.

If a problem needs to be resolved then we work on resolving it, but we don't brood over it until it makes us perennially grouchy and hopeless. Every day, several times a day, we throw out the mind garbage and we find permanent places for the good stuff.

A Quote to Remember

If we think happy thoughts, we will be happy. If we think miserable thoughts, we will be miserable. If we think fearful thoughts, we will be fearful. If we think sickly thoughts, we probably will be ill. If we think only of failure, we will certainly fail. If we wallow in self-pity, everyone will want to shun us and avoid us.

Is giving yourself a pep talk every day silly, superficial, childish? No. On the contrary, it is the very essence of sound psychology. "Our life is what our thoughts make it." Those words are just as true today as they were eighteen centuries ago when Marcus Aurelius first wrote them in his book of "Meditations."[44] (Dale Carnegie)

Think on These Things

Let the words of my mouth, and the meditation of my heart, be acceptable in thy sight, O LORD, my strength, and my redeemer. (Ps 19:14, KJV)

For the mind set on the flesh is death, but the mind set on the Spirit is life and peace. (Rom 8:6, NASB)

Think on these things. Devote your life to them so that everyone can see your progress. (1 Tim 4:15, ISV)

Prayer

Gracious Lord, I praise you that there is more than enough gladness in my life to think about. Forgive my grumpiness and the times I've given in to brooding and fretting about selfish things. Those who love me need to see what it is to think on things that are true, right, and lovely. Transform my spirit I pray, that I may provide them and others with that example. Amen.

38 **Weak Hands and Feeble Knees**
Strengthening Our Grip

> *No discipline is enjoyable while it is happening; it's painful! But afterward there will be a peaceful harvest of right living for those who are trained in this way. So take a new grip with your tired hands and strengthen your weak knees. (Heb 12:11-12, NLT)*

"Get a grip!" This is usually said to somebody who is frantic, out of control, stressed. There are times when we need to get a grip spiritually too. Actually, the whole book of Hebrews was written to Christians then and now who needed and need to get a grip.

In the morning of life, our grip is strong and sure. We have energy to spare. But in the heat of the afternoon, hands get sweaty and tired. Energy wanes; our grip slips. We must find renewed strength and focus to keep going.

Years ago gas pump handles required a tight, continuous squeeze in order to operate. In cold weather it seemed like I needed more and more strength to keep holding that freezing metal handle at the same place. Of course, my grip was just getting tired.

See the runner straining for the finish line: legs getting heavy; lungs screaming in pain; arms pumping; leaning forward; head extended. She's slowing when she hears a scream from the stands: "Go, sweetheart!" Her spirit gets a new grip and she actually accelerates.

Hebrews was written to Christians under pressure. Some doubted whether they could hang on. To them and to us, the Lord sent this message: "Get a new grip! You're going to make it to the finish! I will be with you! I will complete what I began in you."

A Quote to Remember

In poverty and other misfortunes of life, true friends are a sure refuge. The young they keep out of mischief; to the old they are a comfort and aid in their weakness, and those in the prime of life they incite to noble deeds.[46] (Aristotle)

Think on These Things

Jonathan went to find David and encouraged him to stay strong in his faith in God. (1 Sam 23:16, NLT)

Strengthen those who have tired hands, and encourage those who have weak knees. (Isa 35:3, NLT)

[God] gives strength to the weary and increases the power of the weak. Even youths grow tired and weary, and young men stumble and fall; but those who hope in the LORD will renew their strength. (Isa 40:28-31, NIV)

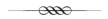

Prayer

Almighty God, you know my frailty in these trying days. Grant me strength, I pray. Sustain me by your grace, and I will remember to give you the honor and the praise. Amen.

39 The Christian's Role
Committing to the Witness Mentality

You will be my witnesses. (Acts 1:8, NIV)

The Lord has assigned to us the role of witnesses. We find happiness, fulfillment, and security in him only as we give ourselves to his directions for living.

Consider the roles of various people in a courtroom: judge, jury, prosecuting attorney, defense attorney, defendant, spectators, bailiff, and witnesses. Religion makes some people hard to get along with because we want to have a role other than that of witness. Judge types want to exercise authority over everybody else. Attorney types feel compelled to prove someone wrong. Spectator types want to be present but not get involved. Bailiff types want to throw somebody out as if they don't belong with the rest of us honest and intelligent people. Witnesses just tell what they have seen and heard.

Consider how we respond to various approaches. We appreciate those who are honest about their thoughts and opinions, who respect us enough that they don't tell us what conclusions we should draw. We resent those who have the attitude that we must see things their way or we're wrong.

From ancient times, one frequent form of prodigal, straying religion is judgmentalism. Satan finds in many hearts a readiness, even an eagerness, to reverse God's order: we apply religious teachings first to others in ways that justify our own behavior, rather than apply them first to ourselves in ways that transform our behavior into Christlikeness.

Quotes to Remember

If we judge ourselves only by our aspirations and everyone else by only their conduct we shall soon reach a very false conclusion.[47] (Calvin Coolidge)

A judgmental heart keeps listening to the things that annoy.[48] (Toba Beta)

Think on These Things

When our reputations are attacked, we remain courteous. Right now we have become garbage in the eyes of the world and trash in the sight of all people. (1 Cor 4:13, GWT)

Work out your own salvation with fear and trembling. (Phil 2:12, KJV)

Remind believers to submit to rulers and authorities, to be obedient, and to be ready to do any honorable kind of work. They are not to insult anyone or be argumentative. Instead, they are to be gentle and perfectly courteous to everyone. (Titus 3:1-2, ISV)

Prayer

Heavenly Father, you are the only judge. Grow in me the witness outlook more and more day by day. Live in me today that I may be courteous and nonjudgmental, I pray. Focus my attention on my own salvation. Set me free of this imprisoning compulsion to be combative and argumentative toward any who see things other than the way I see them. In Jesus' name, amen.

40 A Working Religion
Developing an Active Faith

But watch out! Be careful never to forget what you yourself have seen. Do not let these memories escape from your mind as long as you live! And be sure to pass them on to your children and grandchildren. (Deut 4:9, NLT)

I keep my father's rifle in the closet; it doesn't work. I keep my cell phone clipped to my belt; it does work. I want a religion that works. Don't you?

Papa's rifle is an antique, single-shot 22-caliber. When I got it at his death, the stock was scratched and dented, broken and screwed back together. It doesn't eject cartridges now. I cleaned, mended, stained, and varnished it. It brings up fond memories, but it doesn't help with anything I do today with family or friends, work or play. For weeks it doesn't cross my mind.

The cell phone on the other hand works several times every day. Around the clock it's hardly ever out of reach. There's nothing sentimental about it, but I would be lost without it.

The phone makes a big difference in the way I live, how I make decisions, and how I interact with others. The rifle makes no difference in the way I live. See the difference? One works; the other doesn't.

The Lord intends for our faith, our religion, to make a difference in the way we live, the decisions we make, and how we interact with others. Religion is supposed to work. We grow into it increasingly as the years go by. However, faith can become less like the cell phone and more like Papa's rifle. It brings up fond memories of other times, but it's really not helpful in anything we're doing now with family or friends, work or play.

Our faith may be almost as old as we are. If so, that means it ought to work better now than ever before. So we keep our faith ready to work. We clean and oil it. We keep it charged. We protect the finish, and we keep it with us at all times. It's both sentimental and eternally useful. We'd be lost without it.

A Quote to Remember

Faith is not something to grasp. It is a state to grow into.[49] (Mahatma Gandhi)

Think on These Things

Even to your old age I will be the same, and even to your graying years I will bear you! I have done it, and I will carry you; and I will bear you and I will deliver you. (Isa 46:4, NASB)

You have forgotten the LORD your Maker, who stretched out the heavens and laid the foundations of the earth. (Isa 51:13, NASB)

Do not conform to the pattern of this world, but be transformed by the renewing of your mind. (Rom 12:2, NIV)

Prayer

Faithful Lord, help me to develop a faith that works. Show me how to keep it strong so that it is part of my life every day. Please help me to continue growing in an active faith. Amen.

Footprints
Bible Truths from
Bible Personalities

An idea demonstrated in real life is clearer to see and easier to comprehend than an idea explained only in words on a page. The next sixty devotions call attention to truths that we see in the lives of the Bible's personalities.

41 Abraham
God's Friend

. . . Abraham, my friend . . . (Isa 41:8, NIV)

Through the prophet Isaiah, God spoke these words, calling Abraham "my friend." Why did God so honor this man as to call him "friend"? Consider two reasons.

First, in a good sense Abraham never seemed to "settle down." He began each of the several chapters in his life by picking up and moving at the Lord's command. It's not that Abraham was a restless wanderer; he's just a good example of one who was always open to his God and to tomorrow. From Haran to Canaan to Egypt and back to Canaan, through family dysfunctions within and dangerous enemies without, he kept moving in the right direction, following the Lord's leadership. We need to do that, or perhaps we need to return to doing that.

Second, regarding his faith, Abraham was not among those who retired. His greatest challenge, which resulted in his greatest spiritual accomplishment, came very late in life. God led Abraham through a test that proved him to be the person that some Bible students have called "the Father of the Faithful." Abraham and his wife Sarah had one son, the apple of his eye: Isaac. God tested Abraham to see if he loved his God more than he loved his son (see Gen 22). As traumatic as the experience was, he passed admirably. Surely this test played no small role in God calling him "my friend."

Abraham's great test in his old age suggests that many of us may be in for similar challenges and similar accomplishments in the future. Our God is a jealous God who is not satisfied with anything less than our best loyalties: priority whereby we put God above everything and anything else in our lives.

Quotes to Remember

Where your talents and the needs of the world cross, there lies your vocation.[50] (Aristotle)

Faith is taking the first step, even when you don't see the whole staircase.[51] (Martin Luther King, Jr.)

Think on These Things

The LORD had said to Abram, "Go from your country, your people and your father's household to the land I will show you." So Abram went, as the LORD had told him; and Lot went with him. Abram was seventy-five years old when he set out from Harran. (Gen 12:1, 4, NIV)

You must worship no other gods, for the LORD, whose very name is Jealous, is a God who is jealous about his relationship with you. (Exod 34:14, NLT)

Jesus called out to them, "Come, follow me." (Matt 4:19, NLT)

Prayer

God of Abraham, help me to follow your lead in the events of this day. I don't want to be a restless wanderer, but I do want to be one of your followers. In Jesus' name, amen.

42 Andrew
Mover and Shaker

Then Andrew, Simon Peter's brother, spoke up. "There's a young boy here with five barley loaves and two fish. But what good is that with this huge crowd?" (John 6:8-9, NLT)

Andrew made things happen. Most often he worked behind the scenes, seldom in the spotlight. In this text, it was late afternoon. The huge crowd had gathered around Jesus out in the country, far from any food. As his disciples began to worry about providing supper for so many, several felt helpless, hopeless, and frustrated. Andrew alone suggested a solution: a small boy had a little bit of food. Sure it wasn't much, and even in his hope Andrew struggled with doubt that it would do any good. But Jesus multiplied that food and fed the whole crowd.

We would like to live like Andrew: content to move in the background, offering hope, making positive decisions, and resolving problems.

And in some ways our faith is like his: reaching out but holding back, forging ahead but hesitating. On the one hand his faith spoke: "here's some food." But he was also realistic: "what good is so little with so many people?"

Actually, that's the way our faith always is. We're like the father who pleaded with Jesus to heal his son. When Jesus said that anything is possible to those who believe, the father responded, "I do believe, but help me overcome my unbelief!" (Mark 9:24, NLT).

People who make things happen seldom have undiluted faith that everything they envision will come to pass. But like

Andrew and that father, people who make things happen do have hope and are blessed. They bring their halting, hesitating faith to the Lord. They are positive. They look for a way to move forward. While others are helpless, hopeless, and frustrated, spiritual movers and shakers speak and act in faith.

A Quote to Remember

A leader is a dealer in hope.[52] (Napoleon Bonaparte)

Think on These Things

For I am about to do something new. See, I have already begun! Do you not see it? (Isa 43:19, NLT)

Andrew, Simon Peter's brother, was one of the two who heard what John had said and who had followed Jesus. The first thing Andrew did was to find his brother Simon and tell him, "We have found the Messiah." And he brought him to Jesus. (John 1:40-42, NIV)

There were some Greeks among those who went up to worship at the festival. They came to Philip, who was from Bethsaida in Galilee, with a request. "Sir," they said, "we would like to see Jesus." Philip went to tell Andrew; Andrew and Philip told Jesus. (John 12:20-22, NIV)

Prayer

Lord of everything possible, touch my heart and soul that I may live today in the hope and faith that makes good things happen. Help me to be a mover and a shaker in your kingdom. In Jesus' name, amen.

43 **Barnabas**
In a Supporting Role

> *There was Joseph, the one the apostles nicknamed Barnabas (which means "Son of Encouragement"). (Acts 4:36, NLT)*

Barnabas led from behind, so to speak. Always he was cast in a supporting role, yet the early Christian drama might have fizzled at several points without the parts that Barnabas filled so well. Repeatedly, his actions enabled the young church.

He was one of the first to demonstrate selfless, liberal giving to the church (Acts 4:37). When the church's enemy Paul was converted, Christians were highly suspicious. Barnabas acted as Paul's sponsor, bringing him into the fellowship (9:26-27). When dangerous fear and suspicion arose among the Jerusalem Christians toward the Antioch Christians, Barnabas was the peacemaker sent to investigate and work things out (11:22). When the fledging church at Antioch was growing fast but had no competent teacher, Barnabas brought Paul in (11:25). When the congregation at Antioch became the first to conceive of a missionary trip, who would go but Barnabas? And where could they begin but on Barnabas's home island, Cyprus (ch. 13)?

We also are often cast in low-profile, supporting roles. Sometimes the reasons are logical and apparent; sometimes they aren't. Nevertheless, no spiritually intelligent person is always the leading character. At home, at work, at family get-togethers, in some groups of friends: somewhere every realistic individual is an unobtrusive part of the backstory rather than being the main character. God can do great things through those who play second fiddle.

A Quote to Remember

Our chief want is someone who will inspire us to be what we know we could be.[53] (Ralph Waldo Emerson)

Think on These Things

When Saul tried to meet with the believers, they were all afraid of him. Then Barnabas brought him to them and told how Saul had seen the Lord on the way to Damascus. So Saul stayed with them, preaching boldly in the name of the Lord. (Adapted from Acts 9:26-28, NLT)

Barnabas went on to Tarsus to look for Saul. When he found him, he brought him back to Antioch. Both of them stayed there with the church for a full year, teaching. (Acts 11:24-26, NLT)

Prayer

Heavenly Father, thank you for the supporting characters that you have placed in my life. Forgive me for neglecting to be one of them, and make me mindful today, I pray, of the opportunities I have to serve you through a supporting role. In Jesus' name, amen.

44 Boaz
Giving and Receiving a Blessing

May the LORD reward your work, and your wages be full from the LORD, the God of Israel, under whose wings you have come to seek refuge. (Ruth 2:12, NASB)

Boaz's love story takes place in ancient social customs that often prevent twenty-first-century people from appreciating the deeper spiritual truths in such stories.

Ruth had been a blessing to her mother-in-law, Naomi, when she faced horrific circumstances. As a result of those circumstances, Ruth and Naomi found themselves poor, helpless, and defenseless in a man's society. Boaz had heard of Ruth's kindness, and he became the fulfillment of his own prayer. He married Ruth, giving her and Naomi social standing and security. Ruth gave a blessing, and she received a blessing.

Boaz's kind and godly character brought about his first interactions with Ruth. He gave a blessing by showing compassion for her needs. The result was that God gave him a good wife and a good family. Further, Boaz was blessed to be the ancestor of both King David and of Jesus (Matt 1:5-16). Boaz gave a blessing, and he received a blessing.

God works that way. Those who receive mercy are merciful people (Matt 5:7). Those who receive the Lord's love are those who love the Lord (Prov 8:17).

And the story of Boaz and Ruth is real-life testimony that the path to receiving God's blessing is the path of giving blessing to others.

Today, may we look for people to whom we can give a blessing.

A Quote to Remember

When God blesses us, He expects us to use those blessings to bless the lives of others.[54] (Jim Gallery)

Think on These Things

The LORD rewarded me for doing right; he restored me because of my innocence. For I have kept the ways of the LORD; I have not turned from my God to follow evil. I have followed all his regulations; I have never abandoned his decrees. I am blameless before God; I have kept myself from sin. Trouble chases sinners, while blessings reward the righteous. (2 Sam 22:21-24; Prov 13:21, NLT)

When you give a reception, invite the poor, the crippled, the lame, the blind, and you will be blessed, since they do not have the means to repay you; for you will be repaid at the resurrection of the righteous. (Luke 14:13-14, NASB)

Do not throw away this confident trust in the Lord. Remember the great reward it brings you! (Heb 10:35, NLT)

Prayer

Make me a blessing; out of my life may Jesus shine. Make me a blessing, O Savior, I pray. Make me a blessing to someone today.[55] (Ira B. Wilson)

45 Caleb
Faithful in the Minority

But Caleb tried to encourage the
people as they stood before Moses.
"Let's go at once to take the land," he
said. "We can certainly conquer it!"
(Num 13:30, NLT)

Moses sent twelve spies into the promised land to learn the best way to attack it. When they returned they were 10 to 2 in favor of not going in at all. Joshua and Caleb were the only two who counseled that the people should move into the promised land on faith; after all, God had promised it to them. But they were outvoted. The people did not go in and instead remained nomads for forty years.

Forty-five years later they had conquered most but not all of the promised land. The difficult hill country still had to be taken. Again, Caleb demonstrated faith and volunteered for the task that younger men avoided (Josh 14:12). He was given the hill country, and he conquered it. He did indeed have the courage to back up his words of faith.

Perhaps the most important lesson in this story is the subtle one: when outvoted, Caleb conducted himself admirably. He didn't rant, pout, or sulk. He didn't pick up his toys and go home. He was not on board with the decision the nation made, but he stayed in place. The result was that, even at eighty-five years of age, his opportunity came and he was able to take advantage of it.

Not many of us win every vote. Too often we act like spoiled brats when we don't get our way. Caleb is a good example to remember when we're in the minority.

A Quote to Remember

Humidity's got me; I've started to wilt.
And if I'm not careful, I'm liable to tilt.
My fingers, once nimble, can't do what I ask:
too weak, at the moment, for the simplest task.
Now what was that motto that sounded so fine?
I thought, when I read it, I might make it mine.
"Don't let what you can't do," I think it began,
"deter you from doing the things that you can."
Dear God, grant me patience, and help me rewind.
And please keep me open to the can-do's I find.
Do not let what you can't do interfere with what you can do.[56]

Think on These Things

Don't be afraid, for I am with you. (Isa 41:10, NLT)

I have told you all this so that you may have peace in me. (John 16:33, NLT)

Be watchful, stand firm in the faith, act like men, be strong. (1 Cor 16:13, ESV)

Prayer

Lord of faithfulness, forgive me for the times I've been fearful or have been bitter about not getting my way. Teach me how to be faithful like Caleb, in Jesus' name. Amen.

The Comforter
Sources of Comfort

> *And I will pray to the Father, and he shall give you another Comforter, that he may abide with you forever. I will not leave you comfortless: I will come to you. But the Comforter, which is the Holy Ghost, whom the Father will send in my name, he shall teach you all things, and bring all things to your remembrance, whatsoever I have said unto you. Peace I leave with you, my peace I give unto you: not as the world giveth, give I unto you. Let not your heart be troubled, neither let it be afraid. (John 14:16, 18, 26-27, KJV)*

What comforts you when you are lonely, sad, or afraid? God's Holy Spirit is one powerful source of comfort. We recall some of Jesus' words to his frightened and frustrated disciples on their last evening together: that he would not leave them helpless but would send another Comforter, God's Holy Spirit (see John 14).

There are also spiritual individuals in the Old Testament who took comfort in God's presence, as we see in verses from David's psalms below.

Another source of comfort is our beliefs and doctrines about God's love, his grace, and his power to care for those he loves.

A fourth source is the Bible's "exceeding great and precious promises" (2 Pet 1:4, AKJV).

As we call to mind and repeatedly meditate on these sources of comfort, we find ourselves calmed, strengthened, and uplifted.

A Quote to Remember

Thanks be to God, not only for rivers of endless joys above, but for rills of comfort here below.[57] (adapted from Adoniram Judson)

Think on These Things

Though you have made me see troubles, many and bitter, you will restore my life again; from the depths of the earth you will again bring me up. You will increase my honor and comfort me once more. (Ps 71:20-21, NIV)

Remember your word to your servant, for you have given me hope. My comfort in my suffering is this: Your promise preserves my life. The arrogant mock me unmercifully, but I do not turn from your law. I remember, LORD, your ancient laws, and I find comfort in them. (Ps 119:49-52, NIV)

Humble yourselves therefore under the mighty hand of God, that he may exalt you in due time: Casting all your care upon him; for he careth for you. (1 Pet 5:6-7, KJV)

Prayer

Lord of all our days and of all that is happening, grant us the comfort of knowing that our sins are forgiven, that calm courage and bright hope are to be found in the Comforter, your Holy Spirit. Quiet our troubled hearts, we pray, and lift us up in unshaken trust and faith.[58] Amen.

47 **Peter and Cornelius**
Unlearning Tradition

> *Then Peter replied, "I see very clearly that God shows no favoritism. In every nation he accepts those who fear him and do what is right." (Acts 10:34-35, NLT)*

It was a difficult tradition for Peter to unlearn: that God does not favor one race or nationality over another. The Christian gospel began among the Jews, but it was not for Jews only. God loves and cares for everyone. At first, all Christians were Jews, and they had to unlearn the tradition that God was for them only.

What traditions must we unlearn? We may be able to call to mind modern traditions that respect and honor only people who are like us. Perhaps we have traditions that are built on a narrow interpretation of some Bible verses while ignoring other verses. Maybe we have not examined our traditions in light of Jesus' six "but I say to you" sayings (Matt 5:21-48). Logically, in our minds we easily recognize the disconnection, but our traditions are more subtle.

Traditions can be helpful, encouraging us to continue in good practices and habits. Unexamined traditions, however, sooner or later steer us off course because we misapply them, like a driver who keeps the car moving straight ahead and thus does not keep it in the road when the road curves. We must constantly appraise our traditions in light of Scripture. We must identify the passages that God impresses most strongly on us. The Sermon on the Mount (Matt 5–7) and Galatians 5:22-23 are good places to begin.

A Quote to Remember

The only way my life makes sense is if, regardless of culture, race, religion, tribe, there is this commonality, these essential human truths and passions and hopes and moral precepts that are universal. And that we can reach out beyond our differences. If that is not the case, then it is pretty hard for me to make sense of my life. So that is at the core of who I am.[59] (Barack Obama)

Think on These Things

"You have let go of the commands of God and are holding on to human traditions." And he continued, "You have a fine way of setting aside the commands of God in order to observe your own traditions!" (Mark 7:8-9, NIV)

For there is no difference between Jew and Gentile. The same Lord is Lord of all and richly blesses all who call on him. (Rom 10:12, NIV)

There is neither Jew nor Gentile, neither slave nor free, nor is there male and female, for you are all one in Christ Jesus. (Gal 3:28, NIV)

Prayer

Almighty God, grant that the United Nations may establish that there are no superior or inferior people anywhere in the world, and that there can be and will be equality, peace, unity, among all mankind regardless of race, creed, color, or nationality.[60] (Chauncey Spencer)

48 **Daniel**
A Godly Gentleman Facing Injustice

Daniel made up his mind that he would not defile himself with the king's choice food or with the wine which he drank. (Dan 1:8, NASB)

It's a good ability to have: to make up our minds. Other Bible translations say that Daniel "resolved," "was determined," or "purposed in his heart." Daniel's religion called him to a specific diet, and diet is a legitimate focus of this passage. We're taking the wider focus, however, that we need to make up our minds about life's big issues, giving priority to worshiping and serving the Lord. That's what Daniel did.

Furthermore, he went about it like a godly gentleman. Verse 9 says that he sought permission to observe his own diet. Why be hardheaded and combative about it? Of course, we recall that in a later incident his enemies were successful in getting Daniel dropped into a lion's den because of his religion. We also remember that the Lord delivered him from the lions, and we suspect that his deliverance came, at least in part, because he was a godly gentleman. He didn't get rattled. He didn't fly off the handle.

All too often God's people have a chip on our shoulders. When our faith and habits are challenged, we sometimes get combative rather than remaining faithful in a godly way. Our words repel people rather than attracting them. Meditating on Daniel will help us fix that.

A Quote to Remember

You can tell a man he is wrong by a look or an intonation or a gesture just as eloquently as you can in words. And if you tell him he is wrong, do you make him want to agree with you? Never! For you have struck a direct blow at his intelligence, his judgment, his pride, his self-respect. That will make him want to strike back. But it will never make him want to change his mind. You may then hurl at him all the logic of a Plato or an Immanuel Kant, but you will not alter his opinion, for you have hurt his feelings.[61] (Dale Carnegie)

Think on These Things

The king talked with them, and he found none equal to Daniel, Hananiah, Mishael and Azariah; so they entered the king's service. (Dan 1:19, NIV)

Daniel handled the situation with wisdom and discretion. (Dan 2:14, NLT)

The king asked Daniel, "Are you able to tell me what I saw in my dream and interpret it?" Daniel replied, "No wise man, enchanter, magician or diviner can explain to the king the mystery he has asked about, but there is a God in heaven who reveals mysteries." (Dan 2:26-28, NIV)

Prayer

Lord, you know all too well how much trouble I have making up my mind sometimes. Help me do better at that from now on, as I remember the example of Daniel. Amen.

49 **David**
In the Name of the LORD

David replied to the Philistine, "You come to me with sword, spear, and javelin, but I come to you in the name of the LORD of Heaven's Armies."
(1 Sam 17:45, NLT)

"In the name of the LORD of Heaven's Armies." That's how little David killed the giant Goliath. It's not a matter of saying the right words or repeating some magic formula. It's a matter of living for the Lord, placing all our confidence in him, banking everything on him and his faithfulness.

We must be quick to recall that not every person of faith is delivered from danger in this life. Jesus himself was tortured to death. Stephen was stoned to death.

But faith is indeed the victory that overcomes the world (1 John 5:4). Just as the soldier who falls in battle has not lost the war, David would not have lost the war if Goliath had gotten in a lucky shot and killed David. How often has such bravery renewed the strength of those who stand by, and they have gone on to win the battle?

Not every person of faith is delivered in this life, but every person of faith has signed on with the Lord. Every person of faith is on the winning side.

It's sad and tragic that we often pray for the Lord to make us safe and comfortable, when his desire is for us to find safety and comfort in surrendering ourselves into his hands and doing his will, trusting to him both the earthly outcome and also the eternal outcome.

A Quote to Remember

The purpose of life is not to be happy. It is to be useful, to be honorable, to be compassionate, to have it make some difference that you have lived and lived well.[62] (Ralph Waldo Emerson)

Think on These Things

The race is not to the swift or the battle to the strong. (Eccl 9:11, NIV)

So don't worry about these things, saying, "What will we eat? What will we drink? What will we wear?" These things dominate the thoughts of unbelievers, but your heavenly Father already knows all your needs. Seek the Kingdom of God above all else, and live righteously, and he will give you everything you need. So don't worry about tomorrow, for tomorrow will bring its own worries. Today's trouble is enough for today. (Matt 6:31-34, NLT)

Work willingly at whatever you do, as though you were working for the Lord rather than for people. Remember that the Lord will give you an inheritance as your reward, and that the Master you are serving is Christ. (Col 3:23-24, NLT)

Prayer

Lord of all our battles, you know the scary things I'm facing right now. It's not easy to find peace of mind and certainty about how to think and what to do. Open the eyes of my soul, I pray, that I may see myself in little David's sandals, with audacious faith and confidence. Amen.

50 David
A Pure Heart

Create in me a pure heart, O God,
and renew a steadfast spirit in me.
(Ps 51:10, NIV)

This prayer of David shows us why Scripture honors him as such a great man.

It seems strange. David was an adulterer and a murderer, and yet Paul praised David as a man after God's own heart (Acts 13:22, NIV). Further, the Bible calls Jesus himself the "Son of David." What logic praises a man of such sin as if he were great?

From his balcony late one evening, David saw a beautiful woman, Uriah's wife, taking a bath next door. That lustful look led to his adultery with her (2 Sam 11:2-4).

Apparently the event would have gone unnoticed, but she became pregnant. Uriah had been away in the military for some time, so it would be obvious that the child was not his. Unable to cover his tracks, David gave orders for the military to leave Uriah in a highly vulnerable spot in battle, where he was sure to be killed (2 Sam 11:14-25). That is murder.

But we must also consider that we all are sinners and that God looks at our hearts (1 Sam 16:7), our inward selves. Also, when the prophet Nathan confronted David with his sin, David's response was "I have sinned against the Lord" (2 Sam 12:13, NIV). Shortly thereafter, he wrote our text verse above. Other translations use "clean heart" and "right spirit." This virtue is David's radar signature. This is why he was a great man.

David's response is instructive for us. He understood that the foundation of his problem lay deeper even than adultery and deeper than murder. He knew immediately that his sin was against the Lord and that the remedy was a pure, cleansed heart. He didn't merely ask for forgiveness. He prayed that God would restore him to be again a godly person.

A Quote to Remember

The most professional curse ever snarled or croaked or thundered can have no effect on a pure heart.[63] (Peter Beagle)

Think on These Things

God blesses those whose hearts are pure, for they will see God. (Matt 5:8, NLT)

And this is my prayer: that your love may abound more and more in knowledge and depth of insight, so that you may be able to . . . be pure and blameless. (Phil 1:9-11, NIV)

Dear friends, now we are children of God, and what we will be has not yet been made known. But we know that when Christ appears, we shall be like him, for we shall see him as he is. All who have this hope in him purify themselves, just as he is pure. (1 John 3:2-3, NIV)

Prayer

Heavenly Father, I praise you now as the one who sees my heart, my soul. I ask forgiveness for my sins. But more than that, I pray for your divine touch deep within me, that by your grace, with David, I may yearn to be a better person deep down. Amen.

51 **David**
Envisioning Beyond Ourselves

> *After the king [David] was settled in*
> *his palace and the LORD had given*
> *him rest from all his enemies around*
> *him, he said to Nathan the prophet,*
> *"Here I am, living in a house of cedar,*
> *while the ark of God remains in a tent."*
> *(2 Sam 7:1-2, NIV)*

Perhaps you have known people with the spiritual integrity to work hard for a goal that they knew they would not reach in their lifetimes. Others would reach it later, but these people still gave their time and energy as if they expected to see the completed project. David models that kind of integrity for us.

He realized that his people had built homes (and he had built a fine mansion for himself), but the Hebrews' place of worship was still a tent (2 Sam 7:1-2). This discrepancy touched his heart, and at first he purposed to build a temple for the Lord. But God denied him that privilege, and David's son Solomon is the one who actually brought the dream to fruition (1 Chr 22:8-9). David stockpiled precious building materials: gold, silver, iron, bronze, wood, onyx, jewels, fine stone, and marble (1 Chr 29:2). All along, he knew he would not live to see them come together in a marvelous temple for God.

Living for the Lord often prompts us to lay foundations for dreams that we will not live to see fulfilled. We bequeath character and spirituality to little children who will become adults after we're gone. We model faithfulness for those whose names we may never know, but who will find their way in the future by the light we give in the present. Great good happens through us when we envision beyond ourselves and give ourselves unselfishly to the Lord's work, to his will, to his way.

A Quote to Remember

I have a dream that my four little children will one day live in a nation where they will not be judged by the color of their skin, but by the content of their character.[64] Martin Luther King, Jr.

Think on These Things

The LORD said to [Moses], "This is the land I promised on oath to Abraham, Isaac and Jacob when I said, 'I will give it to your descendants.' I have let you see it with your eyes, but you will not cross over into it." (Deut 34:1-2, 4, NIV)

I sent you to reap what you have not worked for. Others have done the hard work, and you have reaped the benefits of their labor. (John 4:38, NIV)

Those who live only to satisfy their own sinful nature will harvest decay and death from that sinful nature. But those who live to please the Spirit will harvest everlasting life from the Spirit. (Gal 6:8, NLT)

Prayer

Heavenly Father, for our children and our children's children, make me a blessing. In me and through me, lay strong foundations for their spirituality and happiness. Amen.

52 **David's Morning Prayer**
An Undivided Heart

Teach me your way, LORD, that I may rely on your faithfulness; give me an undivided heart, that I may fear your name. (Ps 86:11, NIV)

After the First Baptist Church of Stantonsburg, North Carolina, burned, the congregation and others in the area rallied. One point of encouragement that remained strong long after the rebuilding was completed was the chorus "Undivided Heart." David asked God for an undivided heart, and the phrase appears in several other Old Testament passages in Kings, Chronicles, Psalms, and Ezekiel.

> Lord, I pray for an undivided heart,
> that I may walk the way of truth;
> And may the praise of my undivided heart
> bring you glory, bring you joy.[65]

In Psalm 86, we can imagine King David, perhaps in middle age, at a time when no particular crisis was looming. He prays on his rooftop as the sun rises over the Mount of Olives to the east. In Jerusalem's streets below, the farmers are bringing their animals and garden produce to sell. Shops are opening. Birds sing in the still, clear, cool morning air.

David is a spiritually mature person. His prayers are not shallow or naïve. He is well aware that the issues of life are determined by the heart. Thus he does not pray about any particular matter that is before him today. Rather, he prays for a heart that is focused first, last, and always on the Lord: an "undivided heart."

Life is the same today in that major issues are still determined by the condition of one's heart. Rules and spiritual guidelines are needed, but when the heart is bent on selfishness or sin of any kind, the guidelines are not enough. Along with David, we are wise to ask the Lord for undivided hearts.

A Quote to Remember

Our minds are apt to be divided among a variety of objects, like trickling streamlets which waste their force in a hundred runnels. Our greatest desire should be to have all our life-floods poured into one channel and to have that channel directed toward the Lord alone.[66] (Charles Spurgeon)

Think on These Things

These were his instructions to them: "You must always act in the fear of the Lord, with faithfulness and an undivided heart." (2 Chr 19:9, NLT)

"Remember me, Lord," [Hezekiah] said, "how I have walked in integrity, with an undivided heart, and I have accomplished what is good in your sight." (2 Kgs 20:3, ISV)

I'll give them a united heart, placing a new spirit within them. I'll remove their stubborn heart and give them a heart that's sensitive to me. (Ezek 11:19, ISV)

Prayer

Lord, I pray for singleness of heart to love you and to serve you. Teach me to cultivate David's desire for a clean heart toward you and toward all others. Amen.

53 Elijah
Regaining a Hopeful Outlook

The word of the LORD came to him: "What are you doing here, Elijah?" He replied, "I have been very zealous for the LORD God Almighty. The Israelites have rejected your covenant, torn down your altars, and put your prophets to death with the sword. I am the only one left, and now they are trying to kill me too." (1 Kgs 19:10-11, NIV)

It had been a bad day. Elijah was fleeing for his life. He was so disheartened that he asked the Lord to go ahead and end his life (1 Kings 19:3-4). He was not only hopeless concerning his survival; he also thought that faithfulness to the Lord was altogether absent from the whole country except for him. He thought he was God's last chance.

When we are disheartened, it helps to ponder Elijah. From the tall Mt. Carmel of great victory, he had fallen quickly to the valley. His victory put powerful people in a black mood, threatening to kill him. Often Satan comes on strong just after our mountaintop successes.

The Lord is gentle with us. He knows our frame, that we are dust (Ps 103:13-14). Still, Elijah's viewpoint needed a course correction. In fact, he was not God's last chance for righteousness in the country. There were at least 7,000 righteous individuals left (1 Kings 19:18).

After that, the Lord enabled Elijah to pick up and move forward. He appointed his successor, Elisha, but Elijah himself still remained active as a prophet in more events.

When the roller coaster of our lives dips to new lows, it's helpful to recall that Elijah's disheartened outlook was not accurate, and that by God's grace he was indeed able to find renewal and move forward. We can do that too.

A Quote to Remember

Look not mournfully into the past, it comes not back again. Wisely improve the present, it is thine. Go forth to meet the shadowy future without fear and with a manly heart.[67] (Henry Wadsworth Longfellow)

Think on These Things

The LORD is a shelter for the oppressed, a refuge in times of trouble. Those who know your name trust in you, for you, O LORD, do not abandon those who search for you. (Ps 9:9-10, NLT)

I prayed to the LORD, and he answered me. He freed me from all my fears. (Ps 34:4, NLT)

The LORD is like a father to his children, tender and compassionate to those who fear him. For he knows how weak we are; he remembers we are only dust. (Ps 103:13-14, NLT)

Prayer

Lord of all losers, thank you for loving me and caring about me in times like these. Strengthen me within, like you strengthened Elijah, and help me move forward, I pray. Amen.

54 Elijah
Prescriptions for Depression

Elijah was afraid and ran for his life.
He came to a broom bush, sat down
under it and prayed that he might die.
"I have had enough, LORD," he said.
(1 Kgs 19:3-4, NIV)

Elijah is depressed in 1 Kings 19. In addition to doctors, counselors, and friends, this chapter in the Bible provides prescriptions to help us overcome depression.

We can rise above depression. We have to believe that our God is not pleased when we are incapacitated in any way. God cares, and he wants to help us find a way out.

We must know the signs: fear, exhaustion, suicidal thoughts, delusions, boredom, loss of energy (vv. 3-7, 10, 14).

We must remember that depression normally follows major life changes, both joys and sorrows. Go back to your roots. Elijah is back down at Mt. Horeb. That's also known as Mt. Sinai, where Moses received the Ten Commandments. This is the place of Elijah's spiritual roots.

We must get back among people. Elijah was right to go off by himself with God. But the purpose of getting alone with the Lord is to find strength and direction so that we are able to be back among people. Depression will not lessen as long as Elijah stays in that cave (vv. 15-16).

We must move on with life. It's a balancing act. On the one hand, a great victory or defeat doesn't change everything forever. On the other hand, those experiences often leave subtle changes that linger for a long time. That's normal and okay. We can move forward from there.

When we are depressed, we must remember that we can rise above it; God wants us to rise above it. May God bless us with victory over depression.

A Quote to Remember

Noble deeds and hot baths are the best cures for depression.[68] (Dodie Smith)

Think on These Things

The LORD himself goes before you and will be with you; he will never leave you nor forsake you. Do not be afraid; do not be discouraged. (Deut 31:8, NIV)

The eternal God is your refuge, and underneath are the ever-lasting arms. (Deut 33:27, NIV)

All praise to God, the Father of our Lord Jesus Christ. God is our merciful Father and the source of all comfort. He comforts us in all our troubles so that we can comfort others. When they are troubled, we will be able to give them the same comfort God has given us. (2 Cor 1:3-4, NLT)

Prayer

Lord of grace and courage, lift me out of this cloudy mood. Grant me the tenacity to seek and to find your prescriptions and solutions for today and every day. Amen.

55 **Elijah**
When God Speaks in a Whisper

*Then a great and powerful wind tore
the mountains apart and shattered the
rocks before the LORD, but the LORD
was not in the wind. After the wind
there was an earthquake, but the
LORD was not in the earthquake.
After the earthquake came a fire,
but the LORD was not in the fire.
And after the fire came a gentle
whisper. (1 Kgs 19:11-12, NIV)*

At times, we want desperately to hear a word from the Lord: an explanation, a reassurance, something inspirational and powerful enough to lift us up and out of the lowest emotional depths.

That's where Elijah was. A month earlier he was the super-hero of that great showdown on Mt. Carmel. The 400 prophets of Baal looked silly while Elijah called down fire from heaven to consume the altar they had made. But the valley often follows the mountaintop. We don't get to live up there all the time. Elijah had made an emotional journey from the highest to the lowest. Now he was a wanted man hiding in a cave desperately awaiting a word from the Lord.

Apparently he was looking for God to speak through something else spectacular, like he did on Mt. Carmel. But God does not always speak in the same way. Sometimes we can't hear God because we're looking only at loud, impressive events, while God is speaking in a gentle whisper. That's what happened to Elijah.

A Quote to Remember

God's voice is still and quiet and easily buried under an avalanche of clamor. Often times God wants us to sit before Him in quietness. He doesn't want us to do all the talking. To have God speak to the heart is a majestic experience, an experience that people may miss if they monopolize the conversation and never pause to hear God's responses. The essence of meditation is a period of time set aside to contemplate the Lord, listen to Him, and allow Him to permeate our spirits.[69] (Charles Stanley)

Think on These Things

Who among you will give ear to this? Who will give heed and listen hereafter? (Isa 42:23, NASB)

Whoever belongs to God hears what God says. The reason you do not hear is that you do not belong to God. (John 8:47)

My sheep listen to my voice; I know them, and they follow me. (John 10:27)

Prayer

Lord, we praise you for your patience. Those mountaintop-to-the-valley days shock us as badly as Elijah's experience. However you have to do it, move us toward being able to hear and obey your still small voice as well as the more spectacular ways in which you speak. In Jesus' name we pray. Amen.

56 **Esau**
Too Late for Repentance

Make sure that no one is immoral or godless like Esau, who traded his birthright as the firstborn son for a single meal. You know that afterward, when he wanted his father's blessing, he was rejected. It was too late for repentance, even though he begged with bitter tears. (Heb 12:16-17, NLT)

We do not want to be like this man. In these devotions, we consider more positive examples than negative ones. But for whatever bad examples are worth, Esau is one of the best bad examples anywhere.

Esau was a twin in a dysfunctional family whose story is much too long and twisting to relate here. The point is that in their society, the oldest son, Esau, would inherit the largest share of his father's estate. But he was impulsive and undisciplined. He lived for the moment. He was vengeful, spiteful, and reactive rather than proactive.

It is true that Esau's younger twin brother, Jacob, was not innocent in their dealings. Nevertheless, Esau was not prudent or thoughtful. His willful ways and his unmanageable impulses had a predictable result: he lost or forfeited the eldest son's blessing. The sobering truth that the Hebrews continued to recall for 2,000 years is that "it was too late for repentance."

The Bible majors on grace, on the good news. Still, we are wise to see in Esau the eternal truth that it is also possible for us to cross an internal boundary. Willful ways and unmanaged impulses will have a predictable result eventually, and there does indeed come a time when "it is too late for repentance." This is a man we do not want to be like.

Quotes to Remember

Sin always wounds the sinner.[70] (Caryll Houselander)

Sin is its own punishment, devouring you from the inside.[71] (William Paul Young)

Think on These Things

People who conceal their sins will not prosper, but if they confess and turn from them, they will receive mercy. (Prov 28:13, NLT)

But thank God! He gives us victory over sin and death through our Lord Jesus Christ. (1 Cor 15:57, NLT)

If we claim to be without sin, we deceive ourselves and the truth is not in us. If we confess our sins, he is faithful and just and will forgive us our sins and purify us from all unrighteousness. (1 John 1:8-9, NIV)

Prayer

Forgiving Lord, I confess my willful ways and unmanaged impulses. Guide my steps, I pray, that I may seek your paths and walk in them more faithfully. Amen.

57 **Esther**
Doing the Right Thing

Though it is against the law, I will go in to see the king. If I must die, I must die. (Esth 4:16, NLT)

Wicked Haaman convinced Persian King Ahasuerus to decree that on a given day, Persian citizens could slaughter Jews indiscriminately. Ahasuerus overlooked the fact that his queen, Esther, was a Jew. Esther's uncle Mordecai urged her to go to the king to plead for her people. She protested that she could be put to death for going into the king's presence uninvited. Still, she found the courage to go, knowing that it might cost her life.

History records innumerable great and good beginnings brought about by those who, often under threat of death, did the right thing. Esther's courage was key to defeating one of the first recorded attempts at genocide. To this day, Jews celebrate the Feast of Purim, remembering the history-altering power of one brave young woman.

Not many of us will change the course of history. Not many of us have choices that threaten us with death. But each of us are challenged to speak up at great cost or to play the coward and say nothing. We are embarrassingly aware that not all courageous people are appreciated; many of them indeed pay the ultimate price.

It's not an easy choice. But we have to decide. And we have the ability to choose to do the right thing, like Esther did. If it costs us, then so be it. We must do the right thing.

A Quote to Remember

Have the courage to say no. Have the courage to face the truth. Do the right thing because it is right. These are the magic keys to living your life with integrity.[72] (W. Clement Stone)

Think on These Things

If you keep quiet at a time like this, deliverance and relief for the Jews will arise from some other place, but you and your relatives will die. Who knows if perhaps you were made queen for just such a time as this? (Esth 4:14, NLT)

Mordecai recorded these events and sent letters to the Jews near and far. . . . So the Jews accepted Mordecai's proposal and adopted this annual custom. (Esth 9:20, 23, NLT)

The LORD is for me; I will not fear; What can man do to me? (Ps 118:6, NASB)

———— ∞∞∞ ————

Prayer

Father, grant me courage to live this day for you. There are weak hearts to be lifted up, proud hearts to be cautioned, difficult situations that await a wise word and a courageous character. Like Esther, I draw back from my responsibilities, preferring to ignore the fact that perhaps I am where I am so that I may do the right thing at a crucial time and place. I pray for your grace, that I may be more like Esther in stepping up and stepping out for you. Amen.

58 Gamaliel
Peacemaker Caught in the Middle

The council accepted Gamaliel's advice. (from Acts 5:40)

Gamaliel is unique in Scripture. He was a member of the Sanhedrin (the "council"), the seventy leading religious officials in Jerusalem. As a group they were bitterly opposed to Jesus. Some of them were involved in facilitating his crucifixion.

But Joseph of Arimathea, who helped give Jesus a respectful burial, was also a Sanhedrin member. The Bible recognizes him as "a good and upright man" (Luke 23:50, NIV). There was at least one good person in the Sanhedrin.

In Acts 5, the council is considering putting Jesus' disciples to death. Gamaliel advises restraint. Was he just cautious, or was he able to perceive that the disciples had some real religion?

Another clue is that Gamaliel was Paul's mentor, and Paul was able to do a spiritual about-face from persecutor of the church to missionary of the church. Did Paul see something in Gamaliel's integrity that helped Paul get his own act together?

One legitimate way of looking at Gamaliel is that he was wiser and closer to the Lord than most of his peers on the Sanhedrin, and that he remained a member of that group as a peacemaking ministry. He wasn't caught in the middle. He chose to be there to serve his God.

Whether or not this is true, he had great influence and intrinsic authority over that group. We know this because when they were about to start some mob action, Gamaliel spoke up and they calmed down.

Our family, friends, or group may need such an influence now. When we study Gamaliel thoughtfully, the Lord will show us how to have that kind of influence too.

A Quote to Remember

It is not enough to win a war; it is more important to organize the peace.[73] (Aristotle)

Think on These Things

The quiet words of the wise are more to be heeded than the shouts of a ruler of fools. (Eccl 9:17, NIV)

And let us consider one another to provoke unto love and to good works. (Heb 10:24, KJV)

But the wisdom that is from above is first pure, then peaceable, gentle, and easy to be entreated, full of mercy and good fruits, without partiality, and without hypocrisy. (Jas 3:17, KJV)

Prayer

Lord God, advocate of peace and champion of reconciliation, teach me the way toward peace. Lead me to carry the torch of peace so that congenial oneness may reside always in my heart. Use me as you transform this troubled world into a peaceful state.[74] Amen.

59 The Gerasene Demoniac
Overcoming Religion's "Escape Response"

The man who had been demon-possessed begged to go with him. Jesus did not let him, but said, "Go home to your own people and tell them how much the Lord has done for you, and how he has had mercy on you." So the man went away and began to tell in the Decapolis how much Jesus had done for him. And all the people were amazed. (Mark 5:18-20, NIV)

This man had been so out of control that he could not live with people. He was like a wild animal, unpredictable in his frequent violence. When Jesus healed him, he instinctively wanted to stay with Jesus, to go with him, to live close to him.

When we first come to know the Lord, our remnants of selfishness want to stay close to him every minute of every day. We want to escape the realities of living with imperfect people. Religion, however, is relational. Loving God means loving neighbors. Abandoning the world to be close to the Lord would only exchange one kind of insanity for another.

It is the Lord's intent that we should be living testimonies of his power and grace, transforming violent personalities into peaceful ones and taming the uncontrolled impulses that have made us difficult or impossible to live with. If a physician's healed patient keeps her healing a secret, who would seek healing from that physician?

Religion is not a means of escape from the real world. On the contrary, religion propels us into life's pathways, making us conduits through which the Lord's healing powers touch other people, ushering them into a spiritual springtime of new beginnings.

A Quote to Remember

Never believe that a few caring people can't change the world. For, indeed, that's all who ever have.[75] (Margaret Mead)

Think on These Things

The LORD has done great things for us, and we are filled with joy. (Ps 126:3, NIV)

Wherever [Jesus] went, in villages, cities, or the countryside, they brought the sick out to the marketplaces . . . and all who touched him were healed. (Mark 6:56, NLT)

[Jesus prayed:] "I do not ask you to take them out of the world. . . . As you sent me into the world, I also have sent them into the world." (John 17:15, 17, NASB)

Prayer

Great Physician, I recognize that I still tend to use religion to escape the real world of interacting with people. Heal me, I pray. Tame my selfish impulses. Transform me from one who only loves peace into one who makes peace happen among my family, friends, and acquaintances. Thank you for who you are and for how you are at work in my heart and life. I give myself to you, to be a conduit through which you will be pleased to touch others today. Amen.

60 **The Good Samaritan**
Getting the Question Right

"Now which of these three would you say was a neighbor to the man who was attacked by bandits?" Jesus asked. (Luke 10:36, NLT)

The Lord has a way of turning our questions back at us.

Luke describes the man who started this conversation with Jesus as "an expert in the law" (Luke 10:25, NIV). His underhanded aim was "to test Jesus." When Jesus said that it is important to love our neighbor, this argumentative person's predictable question was in essence, "Okay, so who is the neighbor that I'm to love?" (v. 29). That's when Jesus told the parable of the Good Samaritan to make the point that we need to be concerned more about whether we are neighborly than about who deserves our love. Following Jesus is more about loving others and less about arguing over the finer points of religion, nitpicking about words.

In Jesus' parable, a traveler had been robbed and beaten by bandits, left for dead by the roadside. The first-century counterparts of the modern preacher and deacon came by, and both ignored the wounded man. The first-century counterpart of the modern despised person came by, and he stopped and helped. Then Jesus insinuated that the two supposedly religious people did not obey the second most important commandment of all (love your neighbor, v. 27), while the one supposedly unreligious person did obey, and in so doing demonstrated what godliness looks like.

So, in God's eyes, the question before us today is not "Which person deserves my neighborliness?" Rather, the Lord's question to us is, "Will I be a neighborly person today?"

A Quote to Remember

A man is called selfish not for pursuing his own good, but for neglecting his neighbor's.[76] (Richard Whately)

Think on These Things

If you see that your neighbor's donkey or ox has collapsed on the road, do not look the other way. Go and help your neighbor get it back on its feet! (Deut 22:4, NLT)

The LORD is good to everyone and his mercies extend to everything he does. (Ps 145:9, ISV)

What good is it if you say you have faith but don't show it by your actions? Can that kind of faith save anyone? Suppose you see a brother or sister who has no food or clothing, and you say, "Good-bye and have a good day; stay warm and eat well," but then you don't give that person any food or clothing. What good does that do? (Jas 2:14-16, NLT)

Prayer

Loving and merciful Lord, I pray that you will prompt me to be neighborly to everyone that I meet today. Amen.

61 **Habakkuk**
Does It Pay to Be Good?

Why do you tolerate wrongdoing?
Destruction and violence are before me;
there is strife, and conflict abounds.
Therefore the law is paralyzed, and
justice never prevails. (Hab 1:3-4, NIV)

Every person of love, peace, and good will stands at times in Habakkuk's shoes: blaming God for allowing violence and injustice as innocent people suffer and die while the wicked prosper. Does it pay to be good? Am I throwing time and energy away, like pennies in a fountain? Does my Christian service help anybody stand taller or walk straighter?

The Lord gave Habakkuk several answers. If we are ready to learn, then we can find meaning and encouragement in these three answers. (1) "The righteous will live by his faith" (Hab 2:4, NASB). Martin Luther seized on this verse early in the Protestant Reformation. (2) "They will be held guilty" (1:11, NASB). The wicked never go as free as it sometimes seems. God is still in control. (3) "The vision awaits its appointed time; it hastens to the end; it will not lie. If it seems slow, wait for it; it will surely come; it will not delay" (2:3, ESV).

Habakkuk responded, and in doing so he showed us how to respond also. In effect he affirmed that if the crops failed, the vineyards were barren, and the cattle disappeared, "yet I will exult in the LORD" (3:18, NASB). "God, the LORD, is my strength" (3:19, ESV). In other words, if worse comes to worst, I have decided to trust that God is a just God, that he knows what he is doing, and that he is still in control. Spin it however you will, but I have decided that yes, it does indeed pay to be good. God has said so.

A Quote to Remember

Truth forever on the scaffold, Wrong forever on the throne.—
Yet that scaffold sways the future, and, behind the dim unknown,
Standeth God within the shadow, keeping watch above his own.[77] (James Russell Lowell)

Think on These Things

Your eyes are too pure to look on evil; you cannot tolerate wrongdoing. Why then do you tolerate the treacherous? Why are you silent while the wicked swallow up those more righteous than themselves? (Hab 1:13, NIV)

For the earth will be filled with the knowledge of the glory of the Lord as the waters cover the sea. (Hab 2:14, NIV)

The Lord is in his holy temple; let all the earth be silent before him. (Hab 2:20, NIV)

Prayer

Lord, I have heard of your fame; I stand in awe of your deeds, Lord. Repeat them in our day, in our time make them known; in wrath remember mercy. (Hab 3:2, NIV) Amen.

62 Hagar
The Far-reaching Needle of Ridicule

When Hagar knew she was pregnant, she began to treat her mistress, Sarai, with contempt. (Gen 16:4, NLT)

Hagar was servant to Abraham's wife Sarah. Abraham and Hagar had a son, Ishmael, whom God promised to bless as ancestor of a great nation. Abraham and Sarah later had a son, Isaac, whom God also blessed as ancestor of a great nation. Why then do Psalm 83:6 and other Scriptures name the Ishmaelites as enemies of the Israelites, Isaac's descendants?

One clue is that when Hagar had a son and Sarah was still barren, Hagar ridiculed Sarah. Another clue is that Hagar's son Ishmael made fun of Sarah's son Isaac (Gen 21:9, NLT). The needle of ridicule pierced through centuries. Arrogance is a lively seed, and its sprout is long lived.

There is never any reason to ridicule anyone. Our arrogance always says more about us than about those toward whom we are haughty. Hagar's ridicule of Sarah and Ishmael's of Isaac were certainly not the only reasons for the enmity between their descendants, but neither did it help to create any healthy and godly interactions between them.

Whenever we are tempted to be arrogant and ridicule someone, it's good to recall Hagar and Ishmael. Let us remember how far through time the needle of their ridicule reached, and how deadly it proved to succeeding generations.

A Quote to Remember

We grow tired of everything but turning others into ridicule, and congratulating ourselves on their defects.[78] (William Hazlitt)

Think on These Things

Half drunk by now, the people demanded, "Bring out Samson so he can amuse us!" So he was brought from the prison to amuse them, and they had him stand between the pillars supporting the roof. (Judg 16:25, NLT)

He who despises his neighbor lacks sense, but a man of understanding keeps silent. (Prov 11:12, NASB)

The governor's soldiers took Jesus into the Praetorium and gathered the whole company of soldiers. They stripped him and put a scarlet robe on him, and then twisted together a crown of thorns and set it on his head. They put a staff in his right hand. Then they knelt in front of him and mocked him. "Hail, king of the Jews!" they said. (Matt 27:27-29, NIV)

Prayer

Lord, you endured cruel ridicule and death by torture for me. I love you; I praise you; I give myself to you anew. Remove all arrogance and disrespect far from me, I pray, and enable me to be respectful toward all I encounter today. Amen.

63 The Herod Family
Just Protecting Their Interests

Herod was furious when he realized that the wise men had outwitted him. He sent soldiers to kill all the boys in and around Bethlehem who were two years old and under, based on the wise men's report of the star's first appearance. (Matt 2:16, NLT)

Five different men from the Herod family ruled in some capacity in Palestine from 47 BC to AD 100. Herod the Great tried to kill the baby Jesus.

As heinous as Herod's decree seems to us, it was common practice in those days. Rome ruled the Mediterranean world and required of local kings only that they prevent uprisings. Rome had no interest in justice. So whenever there was a threat of another king unseating him, Herod did what everybody expected him to do: he sought to extinguish all the known contenders.

The wise men told Herod that Jesus was to be born in Bethlehem. Apparently they had first seen the star two years earlier. To be safe, Herod ordered that all the boys in Bethlehem under the age of two be killed. He was just protecting his interests.

In today's world, unscrupulous and ambitious people protect their interests by stealing good ideas from lower-level employees, maneuvering a competent person into an embarrassing position, sabotaging someone's career, and more. It's the same now as it was then. We're just protecting our interests by acting like Herod.

The word "herod" meant "heroic." All the Herods, however, were ungodly and despicable, not a heroic one in the lot of them. They show us how not to live, how not to behave.

A Quote to Remember

A shocking crime was committed on the unscrupulous initiative of few individuals, with the blessing of more, and amid the passive acquiescence of all.[79] (Tacitus)

Think on These Things

The mirth of the wicked is brief; the joy of the godless lasts but a moment. He will perish forever, like his own dung. Those who have seen him will say, "Where is he?" Like a dream he flies away, no more to be found, banished like a vision of the night. (Job 20:5, 7-8, NIV)

A worthless person, a wicked man, goes about with crooked speech, winks with his eyes, with perverted heart devises evil, continually sowing discord; therefore calamity will come upon him suddenly; in a moment he will be broken beyond healing. (Prov 6:12-15, ESV)

God will bring every deed into judgment, with every secret thing, whether good or evil. (Eccl 12:14, ESV)

Prayer

Righteous God, I praise you that your ways are not our ways, that your kingdom is one of justice and compassion. Grant me insight to learn to do good from reflecting on the evil examples of the Herods. Amen.

64 **Isaac**
Treating Children Equally

Isaac loved Esau, but Rebekah loved Jacob. (Gen 25:28, NASB)

Christianity, Judaism, and Islam all trace their beginnings to the patriarchs: Abraham, Isaac, and Jacob. One trait of the Bible that we appreciate is that it does not gloss over the shortcomings of leading characters. All three of these men, along with their wives, played favorites with their children.

Children are destroyed by favoritism. Abraham's sons Isaac and Ishmael, Isaac's twin boys Jacob and Esau, and Jacob's favorite son Joseph all experienced the turmoil caused by parental favoritism. This favoritism is particularly noticeable in Isaac's family.

Esau was a man's man: rugged, handsome, the outdoor type. In their struggle to be born, Esau won out and was born first, with Jacob's hand clinging to Esau's heel. Esau would bring wild game, and Papa Isaac loved to eat it. Jacob was the mama's boy: he was at home around the house, cooking. And Jacob was the conniver, the trickster.

Parents make a grave mistake when we play favorites. It's difficult sometimes to treat our children equally because they are so different: vast differences in abilities, intelligence, likes and dislikes, careers, the friends they choose, and more. May we indeed try our best to treat our children equally, regardless of their differences.

A Quote to Remember

It doesn't matter whether you're the chosen child or not, the perception of unequal treatment has damaging effects for all siblings. The less favored kids may have ill will toward their mother or preferred sibling, and being the favored child brings resentment from one's siblings and the added weight of greater parental expectations.[80] (Karl Pillemer)

Think on These Things

Love the LORD your God with all your heart and with all your soul and with all your strength. These commandments that I give you today are to be on your hearts. Impress them on your children. Talk about them when you sit at home. (Deut 6:5-7, NIV)

My child, listen when your father corrects you. Don't neglect your mother's instruction. What you learn from them will crown you with grace and be a chain of honor around your neck. (Deut 6:8-9, NLT)

Fathers, do not provoke your children to anger by the way you treat them. Rather, bring them up with the discipline and instruction that comes from the Lord. (Eph 6:4, NLT)

Prayer

Heavenly Father, I thank you for the fair and equitable treatment that you give to me and to all your children. Guide me that I may reject favoritism and instead treat all people equally. Amen.

65 Isaiah
Our Divine Purpose in Life

In the year that King Uzziah died, I saw the LORD, high and exalted, seated on a throne; and the train of his robe filled the temple. (Isa 6:1, NIV)

This experience of meeting the Lord shaped and molded the remainder of Isaiah's life. It was his motivating vision of God. He became aware of his divine purpose for living. No doubt he went to the temple that day seeking, searching, open and eager to meet God. We may have such a meeting with God in a revival setting, a normal worship setting, or another setting. Emotional people often have an immediate encounter with God, while more cerebral types find God more logically as they reflect over time.

However it happens, this meeting with the Lord lifts us out of ourselves and plants in our lives a sense of divine purpose. Each of us longs for this meeting. Moses' purpose was freedom for those enslaved. David's purpose was laying the foundations for a nation. Paul's was starting churches. Luke's was recording an orderly account of the progress of the gospel.

Having met the Lord, Isaiah's overwhelming perception was that of a God who is incredibly holy, calling for a volunteer spokesman from among those who are unclean, unholy. Isaiah volunteered, "Here am I. Send me!" (Isa 6:8, NIV)

Our religious experience is unfinished without this sense of call and purpose. Selfish approaches to religion focus incessantly on the marvelous things God does for us. That focus is true and biblical, but it is unsatisfying, like baby food when we are ready for something more substantial. We find our highest fulfillment in saying with Isaiah, "Here am I. Send me!" Seek that meeting with the Lord. He rewards those who earnestly seek him (Heb 11:6, NIV).

A Quote to Remember

The mystery of human existence lies not in just staying alive, but in finding something to live for.[81] (Fyodor Dostoyevsky)

Think on These Things

If you look for me wholeheartedly, you will find me. (Jer 29:13, NLT)

But rise and stand upon your feet, for I have appeared to you for this purpose, to appoint you as a servant and witness to the things in which you have seen me and to those in which I will appear to you. (Acts 26:16, ESV)

So we are Christ's ambassadors; God is making his appeal through us. We speak for Christ when we plead, "Come back to God!" (2 Cor 5:20, NLT)

Prayer

God, I've spent a lot of time and energy in selfish religion, seeking personal assurance and chasing after truth for myself. Thank you for the biblical record of Isaiah's meeting with you. Please guide me to seek that same sense of purpose and surrender to a God who is high and exalted. Amen.

66 Jacob
Building Our Own Altars

There he [Jacob] built an altar and named it El-Elohe-Israel (meaning "God, the God of Israel.") (Gen 33:20, NLT)

Jacob had done a lot of living when he built this altar. He had traveled a long, rocky road of deception and conflict. God had changed his name to "Israel." He had settled for a time in Shechem, having made peace with both his Uncle Laban and his brother Esau, the two men whom he had deceived the most. As he perceived his life calming down a bit, he built an altar to honor the Lord for being faithful to him. Previously, the Bible speaks of the God of Jacob's grandfather Abraham and of Jacob's father Isaac. At Shechem, however, Jacob makes God his own God. The effect of that vital decision colors every part of our lives.

In ancient Israel, the man's decisions were considered the decisions of every individual in the household. Today, we know that every person is individually responsible before God for his or her own decisions. As the slaughter of enemies gave way to loving our enemies, and as polygamy gave way to marriage between one man and one woman, the man's responsibility for the decisions of the whole family gave way to the responsibility of each person for making choices. If God is to be our God, each of us must choose him and commit to him individually.

Like Jacob, many have had godly grandparents and godly parents, but we still must build the altar at Shechem and make God our own God.

A Quote to Remember

The word "God" defines a personal relation, not an objective concept.[82] (Christos Yannaras)

Think on These Things

You are my God, and I will praise you; you are my God, and I will exalt you. (Ps 118:28, NIV)

Then Jesus said to his disciples, "If any of you wants to be my follower, you must turn from your selfish ways, take up your cross, and follow me." (Matt 16:24, NLT)

For God so loved the world, that he gave his only begotten Son, that whosoever believeth in him should not perish, but have everlasting life. (John 3:16, KJV)

Prayer

You, God, are my God, earnestly I seek you; I thirst for you, my whole being longs for you, in a dry and parched land where there is no water. Because your love is better than life, my lips will glorify you. I will praise you as long as I live, and in your name I will lift up my hands. In you, LORD, I have taken refuge; let me never be put to shame. In your righteousness, rescue me and deliver me; turn your ear to me and save me. Be my rock of refuge, to which I can always go; give the command to save me, for you are my rock and my fortress. For you have been my hope, Sovereign LORD, my confidence since my youth. Amen. (Ps 63:1-4; 71:1-3, 5, NIV)

67 Jeremiah
Living in the Now

*And work for the peace and prosperity
of the city where I sent you into exile.
Pray to the LORD for it, for in its welfare
you will find your welfare. (Jer 29:7,
NLT & ESV)*

In her nineties, my mother said that people talk about "the good old days" and how they want to go back. But she had lived in those days, and she said that she didn't want to go back to them. It's normal to long for what used to be.

The Hebrews had been conquered, and all the important people were deported elsewhere to prevent an uprising. Apparently they were listless, drowning in sadness at their loss and anger at their conquerors. Jeremiah wrote and urged them to find happiness in applying their attention and energies to living with present realities. "Build houses, settle down, plant gardens, marry, have children, let your children marry and have children" (from Jer 29:5-6).

In that same book, we find the Lord's much-loved assurances about the future: "For I know the plans I have for you . . . plans to prosper you and not to harm you, plans to give you hope and a future" (Jer 29:11, NIV).

No doubt most of us have never experienced the violent tragedies that the Israelites had experienced: war, rape, pillaging, deportation to a place where the food was strange and the language was unfamiliar. No matter where we find ourselves, we can make today worse by nursing sadness and anger at where we are; we can make today better by working, as Jeremiah wrote, for peace and prosperity. We find our welfare in persistent prayer and work for today, trusting that all is in the hands of a powerful and loving God who promises us a future.

A Quote to Remember

Yesterday is gone. Tomorrow has not yet come. We have only today. Let us begin.[83] (Mother Teresa)

Think on These Things

Do not dwell on the past; I am doing a new thing. See, I have already begun. I will make a pathway through the wilderness and rivers in the desert. (Isa 43:18-19, NIV, NLT, ESV)

Now the God of hope fill you with all joy and peace in believing, that ye may abound in hope, through the power of the Holy Ghost. (Rom 15:13 KJV)

Then I saw a new heaven and a new earth, for the first heaven and the first earth had passed away, and there was no longer any sea. He [God] will wipe every tear from their eyes. There will be no more death or mourning or crying or pain, for the old order of things has passed away. (Rev 21:1-4, NIV)

Prayer

Lord of eternity, I thank you that I have some good memories to recall and a bright future to anticipate. Guide the steps of my mind that I may live well today. Amen.

68 Joab
Living by the Sword

Then King David said to his officials,
"Don't you realize that a great
commander has fallen today in Israel?
And even though I am the anointed
king, these two sons of Zeruiah, Joab
and Abishai, are too strong for me
to control. So may the LORD repay
these evil men for their evil deeds."
(2 Sam 3:38-39, NLT)

King David's General Joab was a violent man. In the verses preceding our text, he had killed Abner, a promising soldier who might have unseated Joab as general. That event made it clear to David that Joab was more concerned about Joab than anything else—especially the good of the kingdom. David also perceived that Joab had too much of a following for David to replace him.

But when David passed the kingship along to his son Solomon, he told him the whole story and instructed Solomon not to allow Joab to die a natural death. So Solomon had Joab killed (1 Kings 2:6, 34). He had lived by the sword, and he died by the sword.

At one extreme is the belief that no violence is ever justified for any reason. At the other extreme is the belief that violence is justified to settle almost any disagreement. Some law enforcement training is said to provide this guideline for the use of force: respond with just enough force to counteract the force that must be overcome, no more and no less. While that is not a perfect outlook, perhaps it holds the two extremes together as realistically as possible.

Still, the biblical outlook must surely favor our striving to be peacemakers.

A Quote to Remember

An eye for an eye only ends up making the whole world blind.[84] (Mahatma Gandhi)

Think on These Things

But if there is serious injury, you are to take life for life, eye for eye, tooth for tooth, hand for hand, foot for foot, burn for burn, wound for wound, bruise for bruise. (Exod 21:23-25, NIV)

You have heard the law that says the punishment must match the injury: "An eye for an eye, and a tooth for a tooth." But I say, do not resist an evil person! If someone slaps you on the right cheek, offer the other cheek also. (Matt 5:38-39, NIV)

Jesus said to him [Peter], "Put your sword back into its place; for all those who take up the sword shall perish by the sword." (Matt 26:52, NASB)

Prayer

God of peace, we worship you as the only one who can see the path through a warring world's troubles. Deliver us from violence, we pray, at the international level and at the personal level. To that peaceful end I give you myself today. Amen.

69 **Job**
Patient Struggle

Then Job replied to the LORD: "I know that you can do anything, and no one can stop you. You asked, 'Who is this that questions my wisdom with such ignorance?' It is I, and I was talking about things I knew nothing about, things far too wonderful for me. I had only heard about you before, but now I have seen you with my own eyes."
(Job 42:1-5, NLT)

Suffering can warp our self-image terribly. The greatest tragedy of slavery is that it made human beings view themselves as unintelligent and worthless. Trouble can sink us in the belief that we're not good people, or that somehow we are to blame for our pain. Sometimes we do make bad decisions, bringing trouble on ourselves, and should accept blame. But the book of Job is not about bringing trouble on ourselves.

It's about holding fast to the belief, when life seems horrendously unjust, that God is good and is in control of life. "Patience" in the Bible often means perseverance and endurance. Job persevered in believing that God is good and believing in his own positive self-image.

Job struggled right to the edge of blaming God for his calamities. All the while, he maintained that he had done no wrong, contrary to his friends' insistence that secretly he must be a terrible person to bring on such terrible suffering.

God was angry and chastised Job's friends for being judgmental when Job needed their friendship the most (Job 42:7,

NLT). God was gentler with Job, helping him see that in his trouble he had lost his respect and reverence for God. Job responded with appropriate reverence and surrender to the Lord. And then God restored Job's health, family, and fortune.

When undeserved suffering attacks, we must resist the temptation to blame God, and we must fight the tendency to lose faith in ourselves. May we cling doggedly to the belief that our lives are in the hands of an all-powerful and all-loving God who is good.

A Quote to Remember

The world is full of suffering, it is also full of overcoming it.[85] (Helen Keller)

Think on These Things

He will not allow the temptation to be more than you can stand. When you are tempted, he will show you a way out so that you can endure. (1 Cor 10:13, NIV)

When your faith is tested, your endurance has a chance to grow. (Jas 1:3, NIV)

If we confess our sins, he is faithful and just and will forgive us. (1 John 1:9, NIV)

Prayer

Merciful Lord of life, I lift my heart to You in my suffering and ask for your comforting help. I know that You would withhold the thorns of this life, if I could attain eternal life without them. Grant me the grace to bear the thorns in union with your sufferings. No matter what suffering may come my way, let me always trust in You. Amen.[86]

70 John
Transformation Needed

We know how much God loves us,
and we have put our trust in his love.
God is love, and all who live in love
live in God, and God lives in them.
(1 John 4:16, NLT)

From "Son of Thunder" to "Apostle of Love," John dares us to tackle the worst elements of our personalities and to overcome them by God's grace.

In the Gospels we see James and his brother John as angry young men among Jesus' closest friends and disciples. We also have seen angry individuals join the church, and the only change in their lives is that they have started attending worship.

In John's letters, however, written later in his life, we see infinitely more than the mellowing that comes with passing decades. He is truly transformed, mentioning some form of love thirty-six times in only seven chapters. Perhaps we need the same kind of transformation concerning our angry spirits, unfaithfulness, fear, or impatience.

(There were several men in the Bible named John, and we cannot be certain that the Son of Thunder and the Apostle of Love were one and the same person. But they could have been the same. Moreover, that kind of transformation is precisely what the Lord does in many lives.)

As the decades pass, we are tempted to make peace with our shortcomings and our sins of personality. John dares us to tackle these faults with the energy and resolve of a fresh college graduate determined to find a good job. Failure is not an option.

A Quote to Remember

Love always seeks for betterment, for ways of making life more workable, joyful, whole, and beautiful. Love examines every option available to bring about an improvement in life. This kind of discernment is an act of decency, not an act of judgment. Rigid philosophies of judgment will seek to establish structure as a substitute for decency, control as a substitute for trust, and the mind as a substitute for higher awareness.[87] (Glenda Green)

Think on These Things

Don't copy the behavior and customs of this world, but let God transform you into a new person by changing the way you think. (Rom 12:2, NLT)

And all who have been united with Christ in baptism have put on Christ, like putting on new clothes. (Gal 3:27, NLT)

Be on guard so that you will not be carried away by the errors of these wicked people and lose your own secure footing. Rather, you must grow in the grace and knowledge of our Lord and Savior Jesus Christ. (2 Pet 3:17-18, NLT)

Prayer

Change my heart O God; make it ever true. Change my heart O God; may I be like you. You are the potter; I am the clay. Mold me and make me; this is what I pray.[88] Amen.

71 **John the Baptist**
None Greater

He must become greater and greater,
and I must become less and less.
(John 3:30)

John the Baptist seized the spotlight in order to turn it toward Jesus. He had courage and humility that are rarely mixed. That's what every Christian, however famous or unknown, is called to do.

Many of us would not have liked John. All who knew him would say he was direct; some would say he was rude. His readiness to point out the sins of powerful people kept him in trouble and finally got him killed. No doubt many of his acquaintances admired him from a distance. But he probably didn't get many invitations to parties for fear he might embarrass the host. His clothes were decades out of style, and he didn't take a lot of baths.

He did have this extraordinary, easy-to-understand virtue: he knew how to get the spotlight trained on himself, and then he was committed to yielding it to Jesus. He was Jesus' cousin, older by just a few months. He may or may not have known months or years earlier that Jesus was the Messiah. However he came to know it, he understood that his task was to prepare the way for the coming of one who would be much greater than he was.

Many Christians face this dilemma: some people like us, appreciate us, and will give us more praise and credit than we deserve. That's the time to stay humble lest we stumble. For all of his pushy traits and rough-edged personality, John shows us how to magnify the Lord.

A Quote to Remember

True humility, the basis of the Christian system, is the low but deep and firm foundation of all virtues.[89] (Edmund Burke)

Think on These Things

Look, I am sending you the prophet Elijah before the great and dreadful day of the LORD arrives. (Mal 4:5, NIV)

For before John came, all the prophets and the law of Moses looked forward to this present time. And if you are willing to accept what I say, he is Elijah, the one the prophets said would come. Anyone with ears to hear should listen and understand! (Matt 11:13-15, NLT)

I tell you the truth, of all who have ever lived, none is greater than John the Baptist. (John 11:11, NLT)

Prayer

O Father, give us the humility which realizes its ignorance, admits its mistakes, recognizes its need, welcomes advice, and accepts rebuke. Help us always to praise rather than to criticize, to sympathize rather than to discourage, to build rather than to destroy, and to think of people at their best rather than at their worst. For thy name's sake.[90] (William Barclay)

72 **Jonathan**
Hands on My Shoulder

*And Jonathan, Saul's son, rose
and went to David at Horesh, and
strengthened his hand in God.
(1 Sam 23:16, ESV)*

Call it a clan; call it a network; call it a tribe; call it a family. Whatever you call it, whoever you are, you need one. Friendships play a big role in personal happiness and also in our effectiveness in the Lord's work. To appreciate this truth, recall individuals who have strengthened your hand in the Lord, as Jonathan strengthened David.

P. G. Stultz stood about 5'4." I heard him say several times, "I didn't come to know the Lord until I was in my mid-forties, so I have a lot of catching up to do." P.G. was a successful businessman, supremely positive, Christlike, always gentle and encouraging. Frequently, he strengthened my hand in the Lord. I recall him as a big, big man.

Richard Moyers is a great Christian. In some tragically hateful church meetings, he demonstrated a consistently Christlike attitude. In public and one to one, he strengthened my hand in the Lord tremendously.

The Lord has blessed me with these friends and others like Jonathan.

Seven chapters after our text verse, we read that David strengthened himself in the Lord (1 Sam 30:6, NASB). It's certainly good to be able to do that between ourselves and the Lord. There's no direct word about this in Scripture, but I strongly suspect that David was able to strengthen himself in the Lord at least in part because Jonathan had strengthened him in the Lord.

We are blessed to find others who are Jonathan to us. And we may be a blessing to others by being Jonathan for them.

A Quote to Remember

A friend is one to whom one may pour out all the contents of one's heart, chaff and grain together, knowing that the gentlest of hands will take and sift it, keep what is worth keeping and with a breath of kindness blow the rest away.[91] (Arabian Proverb)

Think on These Things

Two people are better off than one, for they can help each other succeed. If one person falls, the other can reach out and help. But someone who falls alone is in real trouble. (Eccl 4:9-10, NLT)

I thank my God every time I remember you. In all my prayers for all of you, I always pray with joy because of your partnership in the gospel. (Phil 1:3-5, NIV)

May the Lord show special kindness to Onesiphorus because he often visited and encouraged me. He was never ashamed of me because I was in chains. (2 Tim 1:16, NLT)

Prayer

God, thank you for placing in my life some friends with Jonathan's ability to strengthen my hand in the Lord. Help me do that for someone today, I pray in Jesus' name. Amen.

Joseph
Speaking Kindly

But Joseph replied, "Don't be afraid of me. Am I God, that I can punish you? You intended to harm me, but God intended it all for good. He brought me to this position so I could save the lives of many people. No, don't be afraid. I will continue to take care of you and your children." So he reassured them by speaking kindly to them. (Gen 50:19-21, NIV)

A most difficult time for us to speak and act in Christlikeness is the moment when we are vindicated, and those who had opposed us have been defeated soundly. Our strong temptation is to use our newfound position to make them pay. If we are ashamed to go quite that far, then we are tempted to turn our backs on them and let them suffer without our help.

Joseph's dad favored him and made him a spoiled brat. His older brothers hated him and sold him as a slave to some traveling traders. Decades later Joseph was a powerful man, and one day his brothers stood before him, fearing for their lives. He resisted sinful temptations to get back at them. Rather, he reassured them, comforted them, and spoke kindly to them. Far from having nothing more to do with them, he became their much-needed benefactor.

Their story was full of parental favoritism, sibling rivalry, treachery, lying, and injustice of more than one kind. Joseph's own story was a ragged tale: in an enviable position at first, then in jail unjustly, helping a man who in turn deserted him, and finally gaining a high government position by virtue of his ability to interpret dreams.

Most of our life stories have not been stories of uninterrupted joy and happiness. We too have ragged chapters in the books of our lives. Joseph challenges us to rise above what we have been, to speak kindly, to lift up and encourage people who perhaps don't deserve it. After all, is that not what God has done for us in his Son, our Lord, Jesus Christ?

A Quote to Remember

Only love can transform an enemy into a friend.[92] (Martin Luther King, Jr.)

Think on These Things

But to you who are listening I say: Love your enemies, do good to those who hate you, bless those who curse you, pray for those who mistreat you. (Luke 6:27-28, NIV)

If your enemies are hungry, feed them. If they are thirsty, give them something to drink. In doing this, you will heap burning coals of shame on their heads. (Rom 12:20, NLT)

Don't repay evil for evil. Don't retaliate with insults when people insult you. Instead, pay them back with a blessing. That is what God has called you to do, and he will bless you for it. (1 Pet 3:9, NLT)

Prayer

Lord, who loved your enemies, grant me grace to love mine. And not only to love them but to do good to them. In Jesus' holy name I pray, amen.

74 Joseph
Outstanding People Who Don't Stand Out

Joseph, her fiancé, was a good man and did not want to disgrace her publicly, so he decided to break the engagement quietly. (Matt 1:19, NLT)

As we study Mary's husband Joseph, we become aware of how easy is it for us to take for granted some individuals who do not stand out but who have outstanding godly qualities, like Joseph. In every Christmas pageant, Joseph is in the background. He never has a leading part. He's barely more than a nameless fill-in, a face in the Christmas crowd.

But look at Scripture. He was a "righteous" man (Matt 1:19, NASB). Their society fully expected a pregnant unmarried girl to be exposed, humiliated, and shunned, but Joseph had more compassion than to do that. He "did not want to disgrace her publicly, so he decided to break the engagement quietly" (1:19, NLT).

Joseph also reflected and pondered the meaning of events: "he thought on these things" (Matt 1:20, KJV). He was obedient: "When Joseph woke up, he did what the angel of the Lord had commanded him" (1:24, NIV). He was an honorable man. He "kept her a virgin until she gave birth to a Son; and he called His name Jesus" (1:25, NASB).

Nothing in the Bible even hints at Joseph being anything less than a devout man of God, a devoted husband and loving father. Today we'll probably meet someone like Joseph: an outstanding person who doesn't stand out in a crowd. Perhaps we can be like him too.

A Quote to Remember

A great man is always willing to be little.[93] (Ralph Waldo Emerson)

Think on These Things

For the LORD grants wisdom! From his mouth come knowledge and understanding. He grants a treasure of common sense to the honest. He is a shield to those who walk with integrity. He guards the paths of the just and protects those who are faithful to him. (Prov 2:6-8, NLT)

The godly walk with integrity; blessed are their children who follow them. (Prov 20:7, NLT)

Whoever would love life and see good days must turn from evil and do good; they must seek peace and pursue it. For the eyes of the Lord are on the righteous and his ears are attentive to their prayer. (1 Pet 3:10-12, NIV)

Prayer

Father, Your Word I have hidden in my heart that I might not sin against You; for it teaches me to do justly, to love mercy, and to walk humbly before You. Even when it brings about hurtful circumstances, help me to do the right thing in keeping with the Christ-filled nature I received upon the day of my salvation. May I not be found lacking in integrity but rather be character-ized by my integrity as it honors my Father in heaven. In Jesus' name I pray, amen.[94]

75 Joshua
God Out Front

So be strong and courageous! Do not be afraid and do not panic before them. For the LORD your God will personally go ahead of you. He will neither fail you nor abandon you. (Deut 31:6, NLT)

Moses knew that his days were numbered. The verse above contains some of Moses' last words to Joshua, who would succeed him as the Hebrews' leader. Moses' words carry the weight of decades of experience and a lot of hard-earned wisdom about leadership. "God goes ahead of you," he said. "God will prepare the way."

He was right. The people of Jericho trembled in their sandals, fearing the Hebrews (Josh 2:9, NIV) even before they had crossed the Jordan River to enter the promised land. That's how God works.

When the first spiritually significant meeting between a Jewish Christian, Peter, and a Gentile, Cornelius, was about to occur, both men were skeptical, even fearful. But when they met they were overjoyed to learn that God had been talking to each of them separately, preparing each one to meet the other (see Acts 10). God went ahead of them. That's how God works.

In any task that the Lord calls us to, he leads the way like a shepherd. He goes ahead of us. If there are land mines, or thorns, or any dangers, he encounters them first. From 2000 BC to AD 2000, that's the way God works. So his assurance still echoes down through the vistas of time: "Be not afraid. Be strong, for the Lord God himself goes before you."

When someday we face our crossing over into the eternal promised land, we will recall Moses' words to Joshua, and also Jesus' words to his disciples then and now: "I'm going to prepare a place for you" (John 14:1-3).

A Quote to Remember

Faith never knows where it is being led, but it loves and knows the One who is leading. Faith is deliberate confidence in the character of God whose ways you may not understand at the time.[95] (Oswald Chambers)

Think on These Things

You prepare a feast for me in the presence of my enemies. (Ps 23:5, NLT)

"Go, tell his disciples and Peter, 'He is going ahead of you into Galilee. There you will see him, just as he told you.'" (Mark 16:7, NIV)

The sheep recognize [the shepherd's] voice and come to him. He calls his own sheep by name and leads them out. (John 10:3, NLT)

Prayer

My Lord God, I have no idea where I'm going. I cannot see the road ahead. But I desire to follow you, and I believe that desire is pleasing to you. I know that you will lead me in the right road, whether I see it or not. So I trust that you are going ahead of me, and I will follow.[96] Amen.

76 **Judas**
Control Freak

From that time on, Judas began looking for an opportunity to betray Jesus. (Matt 26:16, NLT)

We can't know for certain why Judas betrayed Jesus. One possibility that fits all the details is that he was a control freak and also a zealot. As a zealot, Judas was consumed with hatred for Roman occupation of Jerusalem and devoted to getting the Romans out. Jesus' talk of being a king excited Judas, but Jesus' thoughts and ways were not the same as Judas's thoughts and ways. So he arranged Jesus' arrest, thinking that would force Jesus to use his divine powers to confront and overthrow the authorities.

If this explanation is true, he never really intended to be a disciple of Jesus. He wanted to use Jesus to accomplish his own plan. When he took the thirty silver coins from the high priests to help them find Jesus, he didn't really want the money. He wanted to be in control. When his plan failed, he threw the money back at their feet.

He finally hung himself, unable to throw himself on the mercies of God. He had to be in control even of his own ultimate punishment for betraying the Lord.

Perhaps psychologists can provide insight into how to handle our controlling tendencies or how to relate to someone else who is a control freak. In any event, we observe this tragic fact of human personality often.

One aspect of a controlling nature is that we cannot give God control of our lives. When the Lord's thoughts are not our thoughts, and when his ways are not our ways (Isa 55:8), we have greater difficulty surrendering to his thoughts and ways. That was Judas. May the Lord deliver us from our controlling tendencies.

A Quote to Remember

The nightmare spirit of control has always been, and is, profoundly stupid. Discovery requires courage and acceptance that we are not in control, and that the future is uncertain.[97] (Bryant McGill)

Think on These Things

Let the wicked forsake their ways and the unrighteous their thoughts. Let them turn to the Lord, and he will have mercy on them. (Isa 55:7, NIV)

As the heavens are higher than the earth, so are my ways higher than your ways and my thoughts than your thoughts. (Isa 55:9, NIV)

The wages of sin is death. (Rom 6:23, NIV)

Prayer

Lord, I confess to being a control freak and to being unable to escape from it. Come into my mind and my personality, I pray, and transform me so that I think your thoughts, walk in your ways, and surrender my plans to your plans. Amen.

77 Leah
When We're Unwanted

She conceived again, and when she gave birth to a son she said, "This time I will praise the Lord." So she named him Judah. (Gen 29:35, NIV)

Leah's dad Laban tricked Jacob into marrying Leah first, then allowed him to marry the one he really wanted: Rachel. Leah was the ugly duckling; Leah's sister Rachel was the pretty one.

There's a heartbreaking account in Genesis 29:31-35. Leah named her sons out of her loneliness and her greatest desire: that her husband Jacob would love her. But he did not love her. So when her fourth son Judah was born she said, in effect, "this time I'll just praise the Lord" (Gen 29:35). No more trying to find her worth in being beautiful. No more trying to awaken love and desire in her husband. No more trying to create her own security by giving birth to sons. At last she turned to the Lord for her sense of worth, love, and security. At that moment she became beautiful, did she not?

Further, it was that fourth son, Judah, who became the child of the Promise (Gen 12:1-3) that was actually fulfilled in Jesus, a descendant of Judah.

This is not a story for touchy people. It's an emotional bog. We've all been there at some point: unloved, unwanted, alone in the crowd, unappreciated, longing for acceptance that never comes.

Leah's story is one of dozens whereby the Bible teaches us to live our lives for the Lord, to find our happiness in serving and praising him.

A Quote to Remember

Loneliness and the feeling of being unwanted is the most terrible poverty.[98] (Mother Teresa)

Think on These Things

I have set the LORD always before me: because he is at my right hand, I shall not be moved. Therefore my heart is glad. (Ps 16:8-9, KJV)

Why am I discouraged? Why is my heart so sad? I will put my hope in God! I will praise him again, my Savior and my God! (Ps 42:5-6, NLT)

Not a single sparrow can fall to the ground without your Father knowing it. And the very hairs on your head are all numbered. So don't be afraid; you are more valuable to God than a whole flock of sparrows. (Matt 10:29-31, NIV)

Prayer

Loving God, there are times when I feel so alone, even with lots of people nearby. Grant me grace today I pray, that I may find joy in your friendship and that I may be the conduit of that friendship to some other lonely person. Amen.

78 **Lot**
A Slave to Impulse

Lot rushed out to tell his daughters'
fiancés, "Quick, get out of the city!
The LORD is about to destroy it." But the
young men thought he was only joking.
(Gen 19:14, NLT)

Lot had lived in such a way that when he warned his family to flee Sodom before God destroyed the city, they thought he was joking. Bawdy jokes lay bare bawdy character, and religious talk was out of character for Lot. He had not lived before his family like his Uncle Abraham had lived. Our calling is to transition from being like Lot to being like Abraham.

Lot always was a tagalong, benefitting from Uncle Abraham's integrity and godliness. When Abraham first left Haran for the promised land, "Lot went with him" (Gen 12:4, NIV). Again, as Abraham left Egypt, "Lot went with him" (Gen 13:1, NIV). Abraham traveled here and there and built altars to the Lord. There's no account of Lot building altars or worshiping the Lord.

But Lot was not just a tagalong. More often than not he was a drain on Abraham's finances, like an irresponsible child who never grows up to harness his impulses. When their two herds became so large that they could not live close together in a land where pasture was sparse, Abraham gave Lot his choice of all the land in the area. Lot selfishly chose the best pastures. That same choice took Lot to live near Sodom and Gomorrah.

Eventually Abraham rescued Lot, first from being the victim captive of a war between local kings (Gen 14:12), and then later from the destruction of Sodom and Gomorrah (19:29).

We have elements of both Lot and Abraham in our spirits and personalities. In the same way that we resist the devil and surrender to the Lord, we also want to resist Lot's characteristics and nurture Abraham's.

Quotes to Remember

The devil's voice is sweet to hear.[99] (Stephen King)

Be good. Do good. The devil wields no power over a good man.[100] (Harry Segall)

Think on These Things

Do not offer any part of yourself to sin as an instrument of wickedness, but rather offer yourselves to God as those who have been brought from death to life; and offer every part of yourself to him as an instrument of righteousness. (Rom 6:13, NIV)

Put on all of God's armor so that you will be able to stand firm against all strategies of the devil. (Eph 6:11, NLT)

Submit yourselves to God. Resist the devil, and he will flee from you. (Jas 4:7, NIV)

Prayer

Almighty God, grant me strength of will that I may resist the temptations of the devil. I'm your property. Throw him out, I pray, that my life may glorify you. Deliver me from Lot-like impulses, and multiply in me the Christlike virtues that Abraham had. Amen.

79 **Luke**
Fulfilling God's Plan

Only Luke is with me. (2 Tim 4:11, NIV)

We have seen individuals who found their niche and seemed to "fit" into life like a hand in a glove. We've also seen individuals who struggled like fish out of water, never finding their calling. Our happiness and fulfillment in life depend on our living in the particular niche that God intends for each of us.

Luke found his niche. Among all the Gospel writers, he undoubtedly was the best prepared to write one for the Gentiles. As a physician, he was educated, could write, and appreciated an "orderly account" (Luke 1:3, NIV). He could also take care of Paul's apparently frequent ailments. At times he was Paul's only friend present. As a Gentile he could highlight the perspectives that Gentiles would understand. The wider Mediterranean world needed an accurate and understandable account of the beginning of Christianity. Having become a Christian himself, devoted to Paul's missionary task and able to travel with Paul to see firsthand what was happening, Luke was the ideal person to write the gospel for Gentiles.

Whether we're thinking about a lifetime, a few years, or the next few days, God has a plan for us, a calling, an opportunity to serve him—our "niche." Identifying that spot and giving ourselves to it is the key to finding fulfillment in life for a day or for a century.

We want to be among those who find our niche.

A Quote to Remember

There are differing gifts. Every one of them is designed, not for the glory of the individual member of the Church, but for the good of the whole.[101] (William Barclay)

Think on These Things

Luke, the beloved physician (Luke 4:14, NASB)

There are different kinds of gifts, but the same Spirit distributes them. There are different kinds of service, but the same Lord. There are different kinds of working, but in all of them and in everyone it is the same God at work. (1 Cor 12:4-6, NIV)

And He gave some as apostles, and some as prophets, and some as evangelists, and some as pastors and teachers. (Eph 4:11, NASB)

Prayer

God of love and life, we give you thanks for your gifts to us. Direct our lives in the ways that best use our unique combinations of gifts. Keep us open every moment to the direction of your Spirit. May we never forget our privilege and responsibility to take full advantage of every opportunity to uplift others by the grace that you have bestowed on us. We pray that you will grant us the motivation to fulfill your plan for our lives today and every day. Amen.

80 Mark
Mending Broken Relationships

Get Mark and bring him with you,
for he is useful to me for ministry.
(2 Tim 4:11, NKJV)

If we have good relationships with our family and friends, there are moments when those relationships are interrupted and then mended. That's what happened to Mark, an outstanding young Christian with a beautiful servant spirit.

We find the incomplete details in Acts 15:36-41. Mark apparently had deserted Paul in the midst of some missionary work. Then, when Mark's uncle Barnabas wanted to include Mark in another work, Paul disagreed. Even Paul and Barnabas went their separate ways for a time. We don't know precisely how Mark failed. Neither do we know when he and Paul mended their relationship.

Subsequent letters of Paul and Peter indicate that Barnabas did find his way into significant Christian service. Paul and Barnabas also worked together again. Later, when Paul was in prison in Rome, in some of his last written words he asked Timothy to bring Mark to help with the Christian work in Rome. So the interrupted relationships were mended.

Mending relationships is seldom an easy or comfortable task, but it's always an important task. Let us think back and recall which of our interrupted or cooled relationships should be mended first. God can help us do this difficult thing.

A Quote to Remember

Friendship is unnecessary, like philosophy, like art. . . . It has no survival value; rather it is one of those things that give value to survival.[102] (C. S. Lewis)

Think on These Things

A friend loves at all times, and a brother is born for adversity. (Prov 17:17, NIV)

As iron sharpens iron, so one man sharpens another. (Prov 27:17, NIV)

Two are better than one, because they have a good return for their work. If one falls down, his friend can help him up. But pity the man who falls and has no one to help him up! (Eccl 4:9-10, NIV)

Prayer

Lord, my friend and I shared smiles and sorrow for a time, but now there's a rift. Please help us get past this. Bring her to my door, or take me to her door, or cause us to meet unexpectedly when we have time to talk. Prepare me to talk with her. Prepare her to talk with me. Please help us put this relationship back together by your grace. Show me the way. What first step do you want me to take? Amen.

81 **Mary**
The Virtue of Pondering

But Mary treasured all these things, pondering them in her heart. (Luke 2:19, NASB)

Reflecting on and considering the meaning of events is a good practice. The verse above follows the visit of the shepherds to the manger the night Jesus was born. Mary must have been thinking about the exceedingly strange happenings. Not once, but three times, Luke tells us about Mary's pondering over the events she witnessed (Luke 1:29; 2:19, 51). This must have been one reason why the angel Gabriel first addressed her as he did: "Greetings, you who are highly favored! The Lord is with you" (Luke 1:24, NIV).

Some people seldom think before they speak or pause to study the options before they make a decision. They have a quick and ready answer for every question and are forever talking beyond their understanding: lots of words but little communication.

They need to learn how to ponder. Wisdom is found all around us, but not by the one who is thoughtless, rushing through life without contemplating hidden meanings. The ant is a proverbial teacher of the benefits of hard work, but only to those who "consider its ways" (Prov 6:6, NIV).

We are wise to make Mary's pondering virtue our own.

Quotes to Remember

It is better to read a little and ponder a lot than to read a lot and ponder a little.[103] (Denis Parsons Burkitt)

Listen a hundred times; ponder a thousand times; speak once.[104]
(Turkish Proverb)

Think on These Things

Go to the ant, you sluggard; consider its ways and be wise!
(Prov 6:6, NIV)

The naive believes everything, but the sensible man considers
his steps. (Prov 14:15, NASB)

Do you see a man who is hasty in his words? There is more hope
for a fool than for him. (Prov 29:20, NASB)

Prayer

God, meeting with you in morning prayer uplifts me and gets
my day off to a good start. I commit to be thoughtful and ponder
the meaning of today's events: to seek to comprehend what you
are presenting to me through conversations, the materials I
read, and events that come to pass between now and tonight.
Grant me Mary's gift of pondering, that I too may be favored
by you and that I may be used to accomplish your wishes both
in my life and in others' lives. In Jesus' name, amen.

82 **Matthew**
The Hated Disciple

As Jesus left the town, he saw a tax collector named Levi sitting at his tax booth. "Come, be my disciple!" Jesus said to him. So Levi got up, left every-thing, and followed him. (Luke 5:27, NLT)

Just by being one of Jesus' twelve disciples, Matthew (also known as Levi) calls our attention to an aspect of the gospel that goes against our human tendency to dislike those who are not like us. The good news is for "the world" (John 3:16, NIV): all people, everybody.

We gather with others like ourselves. But Jesus' dozen closest friends were a unique mixture. Matthew was a hated tax collector. Simon was a zealot who loathed both the Romans and Jews who, like Matthew, worked for the Romans. Peter was a loudmouth. Andrew was more laid back. James and John were angry young men. Others were kinder. And to this collection of widely varied personalities, Jesus said, "Love one another" (John 13:34, NIV).

This mixture of personalities indicates that we are to be accepting of those who are different. It says also that I am not excluded from the Lord's inner circle if I am extremely different from others in the circle.

This diverse makeup of disciples does not justify sin. The Lord wanted Simon to stop hating Matthew, Peter to control his tongue, and James and John to calm down. God hates any form of sin. But he does accept us where we are and begins immediately to move us toward being more like him. That's what he did with Matthew. That's what he wants to do with us.

Quotes to Remember

Ignorance is stubborn and prejudice is hard.[105] (Adlai E. Stevenson)

It's never too late to give up your prejudices.[106] (Henry David Thoreau)

Think on These Things

For the LORD your God is God of gods and LORD of lords, the great God, mighty and awesome, who shows no partiality and accepts no bribes. (Deut 10:17, NIV)

Levi held a banquet in his home with Jesus as the guest of honor. Many of Levi's fellow tax collectors and other guests were there. But the Pharisees and their teachers of religious law complained bitterly to Jesus' disciples, "Why do you eat and drink with such scum?" (Luke 5:28-30, NLT)

There is neither Jew nor Gentile, neither slave nor free, nor is there male and female, for you are all one in Christ Jesus. (Gal 3:28, NIV)

Prayer

Eternally impartial God, bless us with deep discomfort at the half-truths and economic realities that undergird prejudice, we pray. Infuse us with resolve to allow you to work in us to erase injustice and exploitation of human beings made in your image. Amen.

83 **Moses**
Still Learning New Things

But Moses pleaded with the LORD,
"O LORD, I'm not very good with words.
I never have been, and I'm not now,
even though you have spoken to me.
I get tongue-tied, and my words get
tangled." (Exod 4:10, NLT)

When God first instructed Moses to tell the Egyptian pharaoh to let the Hebrews go free, Moses protested that he was not a good speaker. We can't know whether he stuttered, had some other speech impediment, or was just making an excuse. Regardless, God did not disagree with Moses' claim. He gave Moses permission to let his older brother Aaron do the talking. As we read on through the book of Exodus, however, we find that it was not long before Moses was doing the speaking himself, and apparently doing well at it.

We can draw several legitimate points from Moses. First, we can learn to do new things that have been difficult for us for a long time. Moses was eighty years old at the time God came to him with the call that defined his life. Trailblazing has no age limitations.

A second legitimate point is that, if we've been making excuses, God does not accept them. Yet a third legitimate point is that God will enable us to do whatever he calls us to do. We're familiar with the requirement that we learn new skills when we take a new job. The Lord's work also often requires that we learn new skills. So be a trailblazer! Never stop learning.

A Quote to Remember

We learn by pushing ourselves and learning what really lies at the outer reaches of our abilities.[107] (Josh Waitzkin)

Think on These Things

Intelligent people are always ready to learn. Their ears are open for knowledge. (Prov 18:15, NLT)

Rather, speaking the truth in love, we are to grow up in every way into him who is the head, into Christ. (Eph 4:15, ESV)

Grow in the grace and knowledge of our Lord and Savior Jesus Christ. (2 Pet 3:18, NIV)

Prayer

God, I pray that you will continue to give me the Spirit of wisdom, that the eyes of my understanding will be enlightened. I pray that the same mighty power which You worked in Christ when You raised Him from the dead and seated Him at Your right hand in the heavenly places, far above all principality, power, might, dominion and every name, is working inside of me. I thank You, Father, for Your grace which was given to me by Christ Jesus, that I will continue to be enriched in everything by You, in all utterance and all knowledge, so that I come short in no gift.[108] Amen.

84 Paul
About-face!

"Who are you, Lord?" Saul asked. "I am Jesus, whom you are persecuting," he replied. "Now get up and go into the city, and you will be told what you must do." (Acts 9:5-6, NIV)

Paul (Saul) was the worst at first, but he became the best at last. Earlier in life he lived out a supreme contradiction, super religious on the one hand and persecuting godly people on the other hand. His was an essentially ungodly spirit overlaid with religious credentials.

Paul was a highly respected young Pharisee. He was Christians' worst nightmare, throwing them in prison, watching and approving the stoning of deacon Stephen (Acts 7:58). His was that terrible, awesome, and peculiar kind of hatred dressed in religious clothes and religious terminology. It's arrogant, malicious, and spiritually nasty.

When Paul met the Lord, however, he did an about-face: a complete reversal from persecutor to missionary. He didn't just give up his old ways; he became an activist for the Lord and for the Christian church. And he wasn't just one of many Christian activists; he became the point of the spear in the gospel's advance throughout the Mediterranean world.

Those of us who, like Paul, are religious but ungodly, can change dramatically. It's possible for others we know to experience the same change when they finally meet the Lord they've been talking about so much. New Testament grace can replace Old Testament fury.

Most of us weren't as bad as Paul before or as good as Paul after, but we each need to do a self-assessment from time to time. We want to be like Paul after, not like Paul before.

A Quote to Remember

True salvation is freedom from negativity.[109] (Ekhart Tolle)

Think on These Things

Fret not yourself because of evildoers; be not envious of wrong-doers! For they will soon fade like the grass and wither like the green herb. (Ps 37:1-2, ESV)

And let us not grow weary of doing good, for in due season we will reap, if we do not give up. So then, as we have opportunity, let us do good to everyone, and especially to those who are of the household of faith. (Gal 6:9-10, ESV)

Be kind to one another, tenderhearted, forgiving one another, as God in Christ forgave you. (Eph 4:32, ESV)

Prayer

Dear Jesus, help me to spread your fragrance everywhere I go. Flood my soul with your spirit and life. Penetrate and possess my whole being so completely that my life may be a reflection of yours. Live in me, that everyone with whom I come into contact may feel your presence within me. Let them look up and see no longer me, but only Jesus. Amen.[110]

85 **Peter**
Increasing in Reverence

Be holy in everything you do.
(1 Pet 1:15)

From Peter we learn that some dedicated followers of the Lord still need to increase in reverence for God as the years pass. Immediately after Peter's great confession of faith at Caesarea Philippi, he rebuked Jesus for saying that Jesus would suffer at the hands of his enemies (Matt 16:13-23). Peter's idea of God's Messiah did not include his suffering, so he proceeded to correct Jesus. What colossal, blind arrogance, to try to tell the Lord himself what he can or cannot do! At that point he was not open to the possibility of anything that was beyond his comprehension. For him, God had to fit inside the tiny cup of Peter's understanding.

Fast forward years later to when Peter wrote his letters. He had learned to be more reverent. In addition to our Scripture, he wrote that we should live in reverent fear of the Lord (1 Pet 1:17). We can imagine him writing these words and shaking his head in amazement as he remembered and wondered how he could ever have been so rude to the Lord.

He wrote also that we must stay vigilant (1 Pet 5:8) because the devil is like a roaring lion looking for someone to devour. Perhaps he remembered falling asleep while Jesus prayed the night he was arrested. He was devoured by irreverence and inattentiveness. But he grew in the Lord. He became more holy as the years passed. We can do that too.

A Quote to Remember

Saints and angels behold that glory of God which consists in the beauty of His holiness; and it is this sight only that will melt and humble the hearts of men, wean them from the world, draw them to God, and effectually change them. A sight of the awful greatness of God may overpower men's strength, and be more than they can endure; but if the moral beauty of God be hid, the enmity of the heart will remain in its full strength. But the first glimpse of the moral and spiritual glory of God shining into the heart produces all these effects as it were with omnipotent power, which nothing can withstand.[111] (Jonathan Edwards)

Think on These Things

It is the LORD your God you must follow, and him you must revere. Keep his commands and obey him; serve him and hold fast to him. (Deut 13:4, NIV)

Show proper respect to everyone, love the family of believers, fear God, honor the emperor. (1 Pet 2:17, NIV)

Always being ready to make a defense to everyone who asks you to give an account for the hope that is in you, yet with gentleness and reverence. (1 Pet 3:15, NASB)

Prayer

Breathe in me, O Holy Spirit, that my thoughts may all be holy. Act in me, O Holy Spirit, that my work, too, may be holy. Guard me, O Holy Spirit, so that I may always be holy. Amen.

86 Peter
Following at a Distance

Then all the disciples deserted him and fled . . . but Peter followed him at a distance. (Matt 26:57-58, NIV)

We want to live as close to the Lord as possible. Our text brings an interesting picture to mind. The larger picture is that at Jesus' arrest, all his disciples abandoned him, "fled." But the more careful detail shows Peter following perhaps fifty or one hundred yards behind. He didn't know what to do. He had tried to defend Jesus and Jesus had rebuked him, telling him to put his weapon away. So he couldn't rush in and try again to rescue the Lord. But neither did he want to check out and disappear. When we're off balance, often we are with Peter, following at a distance.

Peter was off balance because Jesus had not appreciated his courageous defense. Elijah was off balance because, just after the great spiritual victory at Mt. Carmel, the queen wanted him killed and God was not intervening. Habakkuk was off balance because he couldn't understand why God allowed the wicked to prosper. Most often when we're off balance spiritually, it has something to do with God not acting the way we think he ought to act. Those are the times we find ourselves with Peter: not really deserting Jesus but not staying near to him either. We follow "at a distance."

A few pages later we find Peter close to the Lord again. To condense the details, he wanted to be there. It's the "want to" that makes the difference, that enables us to rebalance, revive, be renewed, recover our close walk with the Lord.

While it's not a flattering state to be in (following Jesus at a distance), we can understand. We've all been there. Blessed are they who want to be close with the Lord again, for those who draw near to the Lord find him drawing near to them (Jas 4:8, NIV).

A Quote to Remember

Saints are only sinners who keep on going.[112]

Think on These Things

The righteous keep moving forward, and those with clean hands become stronger and stronger. (Job 17:9, NLT)

Let us not become weary in doing good, for at the proper time we will reap a harvest if we do not give up. (Gal 6:9, NIV)

Come close to God, and God will come close to you. (Jas 4:8, NLT)

Prayer

Eternal Father, thank you for your patience in forgiving me time and again as I've gotten off balance when you do things your way and not mine. Strengthen me, I pray, that I may not follow at a distance but may instead draw close to you. Amen.

87 **Pharaoh**
Playing God

Pharaoh said, "Who is the LORD that I should obey His voice? I do not know the LORD." (Exod 5:2, NASB)

The Egyptian pharaohs were thought to be gods. In life they ruled over the living. In death they were thought to rule over the dead. Understandably, we don't read much about rebellions and revolutions in ancient Egypt!

Some of the Roman emperors were also considered to be gods. By some accounts, they did not demand this honor. Rather it was thrust upon them by subjects who wanted to believe that their rulers were divine. This human claim to be divine is not unusual in history.

The term "pharaoh" was applied to all of Egypt's ancient kings, as the term "president" is applied to the head of the executive branch in the American government. The word "pharaoh" meant something like "his honor" or "his majesty." It was a title, and each pharaoh also had a personal name.

Essentially, playing God means that I think that I'm the boss; there's no one who can tell me what to do. That's the mindset in the verse above.

Another common Christian failure is acting like I'm right, and therefore I'm with God, so if you disagree with me then you're not with God and you're wrong. That's playing God.

While few or none of us ever make the outward claim to be divine as Pharaoh did, we are tempted to act like we are. We sometimes act like our possessions and our decisions are ours to do with as we please; we act like the world is ours to trash if we want to. That's playing God.

Today, let God be God. Let us be his servants.

A Quote to Remember

Faith, as Paul saw it, was a living, flaming thing leading to surrender and obedience to the commandments of Christ.[113] (A. W. Tozer)

Think on These Things

Be still, and know that I am God. I will be exalted among the nations, I will be exalted in the earth! (Ps 46:10, ESV)

Trust in the Lord with all your heart, and do not lean on your own understanding. In all your ways acknowledge him, and he will make straight your paths. (Prov 3:5-6, ESV)

I appeal to you therefore, brothers, by the mercies of God, to present your bodies as a living sacrifice, holy and acceptable to God, which is your spiritual worship. (Rom 12:1, ESV)

Prayer

Heavenly Father, I worship you as the one who has rightful control of my life. At times I get it right by giving over to you, and then there are other times. Forgive me, I pray. Guide my steps and my thoughts today, that I may not fail to seek your will before I speak or act. Thank you for the gift of this day, and I give it back to you. Amen.

88 Pilate
Reputation

He ordered Jesus flogged with a lead-tipped whip, then turned him over to the Roman soldiers to be crucified.
(Mark 15:15, NLT)

Bad reputations aren't always deserved, but they stick around anyway. Pilate will forever be remembered, and rightfully so, as the one who sentenced Jesus to die on the cross.

Luke wrote that Pilate "had decided to release [Jesus]" (Acts 3:13, NASB). The Gospel of Matthew also pictures Pilate as a man looking for some way not to crucify Jesus. At the Passover feast, Pilate normally released one prisoner. The choice he gave to the mob was whether they wanted him to release Jesus or the notorious Barabbas. It would seem that Pilate hoped they would want Barabbas punished and Jesus released, but they wanted Jesus crucified. Pilate asked what evil Jesus had done. Still, they screamed and yelled for his crucifixion. Pilate responded, "He is not guilty of any crime" (John 18:38, NLT). But at last he washed his hands before the mob, symbolically refusing to accept responsibility for Jesus' death.

There are several accounts of what happened to Pilate after that day. One account is that he lived in several different places, gradually was overcome by his guilt, and finally hanged himself.

Pilate may not have been completely bad. But there was a time when he cast his lot with Rome and committed himself to doing whatever it took to prevent riots rather than dispensing justice. When it was time to decide about Jesus, Pilate honored not the truth but his Roman commitment.

We all get caught in sticky situations when there seems to be no good answer, yet those are the times that often determine a reputation for decades and centuries. When decision time comes for us, we don't want to be boxed in by previous commitments to cast our lot with someone other than the Lord. We want to be free to do the right thing. Today is the day to avoid following in Pilate's sad footsteps. Today, cast your lot with the Lord.

A Quote to Remember

The risk of a wrong decision is preferable to the terror of indecision.[114] (Maimonides)

Think on These Things

Elijah came near to all the people and said, "How long will you hesitate between two opinions? If the LORD is God, follow Him; but if Baal, follow him." (1 Kgs 18:21, NASB)

No man can serve two masters: for he will hate the one, and love the other; or else he will hold to the one, and despise the other. Ye cannot serve God and mammon. (Matt 6:24, KJV)

An indecisive man is unstable in all his ways. (Jas 1:8, HCSB)

Prayer

Almighty God, shed light on my thoughts that I may see which decision is right. Help me concentrate, think objectively, see your will clearly, and decide as your child.[115] Amen.

89 **The Prodigal Son**
Coming to Our Senses

The younger son gathered everything
together and went on a journey
into a distant country, and there he
squandered his estate with loose living.
(Luke 15:13, NASB)

We call him a prodigal because he did not respect his father, his inheritance, or himself, and because he "wasted all his money on wild living" (Luke 15:13, NLT). He symbolizes our animal urges: self-centered, short sighted, brazenly grasping, living for the moment, doing whatever feels good without regard for the consequences, naïve and unrealistic.

He stands as a warning to us when we get in that prodigal frame of mind, either in youth or at any other time in life. Some prodigals try to blame somebody else for their calamities. In most families, communities, and far countries, there is indeed more than enough blame to go around, but the prodigal brought his troubles on himself. His descent into the pigpen was his own doing. But he wisely concluded those embarrassing pages and started a new chapter.

He stands also as a hopeful prospect for us if we find ourselves at the bottom, in the gutter, in the pigpen today. He was able to get a redeeming point of view. His dad received him back with open arms. There is for us, as Jeremiah said to a prodigal nation, "a future and hope" (Jer 29:11, NLT).

Finally, the prodigal stands as a leveling influence to those of us who have prodigal sons, daughters, friends, or other loved ones. Not all of them die in oblivion. Some recall a Christian's words, the testimony of a godly person. They finally "come to their senses" (Luke 15:17, NIV) and reverse their prodigal path. That's what we pray for.

A Quote to Remember

Never cease loving a person, and never give up hope, for even the prodigal son who had fallen most low, could still be saved; the bitterest enemy and also he who was your friend could again be your friend; love that has grown cold can kindle again.[116] (Søren Kierkegaard)

Think on These Things

Train up a child in the way he should go: and when he is old, he will not depart from it. (Prov 22:6, NIV)

I will give them a heart to know me, that I am the LORD. They will be my people, and I will be their God, for they will return to me with all their heart. (Jer 24:7, NIV)

I myself will search for my sheep. As a shepherd looks after his scattered flock, so I will rescue them from all the places where they were scattered. (from Ezek 34:11-12, NIV)

Prayer

Loving Father, I praise you for your wisdom and patience with me and other prodigals. Thank you for receiving me with open arms when I was so undeserving. I pray now for other prodigals, that you will be at work in their hearts so they might come to their senses. On those few occasions when I'm able to interact, please grant me your wisdom. Amen.

90 Rebekah
Why Me?

The babies jostled each other within her, and she said, "Why is this happening to me?" So she went to inquire of the LORD. (Gen 25:22, NIV)

We all ask sometimes, "Why me, Lord?" "If all is well, why am I like this?" (Gen 25:22, KJV). Rebekah knew she was pregnant. They had no ultrasound, so she didn't know she carried twins or what gender they were. With understandable alarm, she wondered if her abnormal symptoms signaled a problem with her pregnancy. The Lord explained to her that her twin boys would become nations at odds with each other, and even in the womb they were fighting.

Not many of us have been pregnant with fighting twins, but all of us wonder, "If everything is okay, why do I feel so not okay?" First, we must recognize that something is indeed wrong: an abscessed tooth, a viral infection, chronic depression. When life seems to be falling apart, it's not always God at work in us. Sometimes it's another force.

But sometimes God's activity in us can indeed bring us to Rebekah's question, and it's good to realize that before it happens so we aren't thrown off balance. Friendships sometimes develop in unhealthy spiritual ways, and we must allow them to cool or come to an end. Honesty in business may mean that someone else gets ahead in the world's measure. If we maintain integrity in the workplace, we may find ourselves in situations that are not okay.

Rebekah modeled for us what to do with that question when it burns itself into our minds: "she went to ask the LORD about it." That's a good reflex response to cultivate—as a submissive child of God, we seek him out and look for his direction.

A Quote to Remember

Why me Lord? What have I ever done
to deserve even one of the pleasures I've known?
Tell me Lord; what did I ever do t
hat was worth loving you, or the kindness you've shown?[117]

Think on These Things

Trust in the Lord and do good; dwell in the land and enjoy safe pasture. (Ps 37:3, NIV)

Seek the Lord while you can find him. Call on him now while he is near. (Isa 55:6, NLT)

And we know that God causes everything to work together for the good of those who love God and are called according to his purpose for them. (Rom 8:28, NLT)

Prayer

Lord, my mind gets off balance in hard times. I start blaming everybody else, even you. Forgive me, I pray. Help me to respond to all of the things that are happening so that I may grow stronger in faith and in the trust that you are working it all together for good. Amen.

91 The Rich Young Ruler
Heaven's Price Tag

Jesus told him, "If you want to be perfect, go and sell all your possessions and give the money to the poor, and you will have treasure in heaven. Then come, follow me." (Matt 19:21, NLT)

The rich young ruler was admirable in many ways. We would be pleased for our granddaughter to marry him. But he was essentially a self-centered person in religious guise. Notice what he did not ask. He didn't ask, "How can I serve God best?" He didn't ask, "How can I be of the greatest benefit to others?" His question centered on himself because his priorities were self-centered. He was not particularly interested in becoming the kind of person who gains heaven; he was merely interested in gaining heaven. In fact, he thought he could buy his way in. In spite of all his holy talk, he was still storing up treasure here on earth.

The most accurate assessment of his character and his religion is this: he wanted to know how much it would cost him to add heaven to his portfolio.

Jesus' final answer was insightful. If the man had been most attached to his family, Jesus might have said, "You must hate everyone else by comparison: your father and mother, wife and children, brothers and sisters" (Luke 14:26, NLT).

Some Bible students miss the point here and think that the Lord would have all of us sell everything we have and give it away. The main point is that whatever stands between us and the Lord is what we must move down in our list of priorities. We must strive to put the Lord at the top.

So what is heaven's price tag? In one way of looking at it, heaven costs everything we have. In another way of looking at it, it's a trick question, a wrong-headed question. Heaven is actually a by-product of a heart and life that gives the Lord first place in everything.

A Quote to Remember

Heaven wheels above you, displaying to you her eternal glories, and still your eyes are on the ground.[118] (Dante Alighieri)

Think on These Things

Don't store up treasures here on earth, where moths eat them and rust destroys them, and where thieves break in and steal. Store your treasures in heaven, where moths and rust cannot destroy, and thieves do not break in and steal. (Matt 6:19-21, NLT)

The person without the Spirit does not accept the things that come from the Spirit of God but considers them foolishness, and cannot understand them. (1 Cor 2:14, NIV)

Set your hearts on things above, where Christ is. (Col 3:1, NIV)

Prayer

Lord, help me to store up treasure in heaven. I want to be the kind of person who will be welcome there. In Jesus' holy name I pray, amen.

92 Ruth
God's Inclusive Grace

This is the genealogy of Jesus the Messiah the son of David, the son of Abraham: . . . Salmon the father of Boaz, whose mother was Rahab, Boaz the father of Obed, whose mother was Ruth, Obed the father of Jesse, and Jesse the father of King David.
(Matt 1:1, 5-6, NIV)

At our first reading of the short little book of Ruth, a question arises: why is this story in the Bible? These people are only superficially religious; there are only a few shallow mentions of the Lord; there are no altars and no sacrifices in the whole story.

It's there to show God's grace that includes all people. The Hebrews were descended from Abraham, and they had a word for everybody else: "Gentiles." The word was said with a sneer, like Romans spoke the word "barbarian," like Americans may speak the words that refer to certain races or nationalities. Ruth was descended from Moab, the product of Lot's incestuous relation with his daughter (Gen 19:37). Ruth therefore was a Gentile, and Moabites were particularly detestable to Hebrews.

The book's most important lesson is the least obvious: Jesus had Gentile blood in his veins. Gentile Ruth was King David's great-grandmother, and therefore an ancestor of Jesus himself. As God prepared to send the Messiah, he set events up so that Jesus would not only be saying that God cares for Gentiles. He himself would also be a living parable of that fact.

If some arrogant, exclusive religious people have made us feel small and insignificant, Ruth's story is a welcome word. We do not have to join arrogant and exclusive religious clubs to become God's children. His grace includes people like Ruth and people like us.

The other side of that coin is that when we are tempted to be contemptuous of someone, Ruth reminds us that God loves the people whom we find unlovely, so we need to keep working to appreciate and value them.

A Quote to Remember
Red and yellow, black and white: all are precious in his sight.[119]

Think on These Things
For God so loved the world . . . . (John 3:16, KJV)

I have other sheep, too, that are not in this sheepfold. I must bring them also. They will listen to my voice, and there will be one flock with one shepherd. (John 10:16, NLT)

For there is no difference between Jew and Gentile; the same Lord is Lord of all and richly blesses all who call on him. (Rom 10:12, NIV)

Prayer
One God of all, our thanks and praise belong to you, the source of all being. In you we live, move, and have our being, O Lord! And by your sovereign grace alone, we receive salvation and wholeness in you. We thank you for the inclusive life and compassionate teachings of Jesus our Lord. We pray for grace to live out that compassion to all today. Amen.[120]

93 **Samson**
Enslaved to Vengeance

*Samson prayed, "Sovereign Lord,
remember me again. O God, please
strengthen me just one more time. Let
me pay back the Philistines for the loss
of my two eyes." (Judg 16:28, NLT)*

More than anybody else in the Bible, Samson seems to have
been driven by vengeance. Other than his physical urges, he
had no goals or priorities aside from getting back at whoever
had offended him most recently. He had an itchy trigger finger.

His last weeks bordered on torturous: captured, his eyes
gouged out, harnessed to turn a mill wheel in sunshine and rain
with frequent taunts from his captors. That experience might
have humbled another man, but it only fuelled Samson's rage
for vengeance. His final act took the lives of more Philistines in
his death than he had killed in his life. His final prayer was for
strength to avenge the gouging out of his eyes (Judg 16:28). He
was an erupting volcano of vengeance.

Among the passions that destroy the image of God in us,
vengeance may be less common, but it can be nonetheless
complete in its damage. It takes us down to the level of the one
who injured us rather than lifts us above him. Vengeance maims
good character. Someone has said that when we harbor revenge,
happiness will dock elsewhere.

If a wrong needs to be set right, then we should conduct
ourselves as to the Lord. Take positive steps. Move people and
issues toward resolution. First, we should conquer the inner
impulse to dwell on bitterness and revenge. Then, we must

speak or act according to the Lord's direction to accomplish something good. Don't be a Samson.

A Quote to Remember

By taking revenge, a man is but even with his enemy; but in passing over it, he is superior.[121] (Francis Bacon)

Think on These Things

Dear friends, never take revenge. Leave that to the righteous anger of God. For the Scriptures say, "I will take revenge; I will pay them back," says the Lord. (Rom 12:19, NLT)

You have heard that it was said, "Eye for eye, and tooth for tooth." But I tell you, do not resist an evil person. If anyone slaps you on the right cheek, turn to them the other cheek also. (Matt 5:38-42, NIV)

For we know him who said, "It is mine to avenge; I will repay," and again, "The Lord will judge his people." It is a dreadful thing to fall into the hands of the living God. (Heb 10:30-31, NIV)

Prayer

Great God, save us from ourselves, from the vengeance in our hearts. Forgive us for giving way to bitterness and planning to return hurt for hurt, terror for terror. We beg of you to grant us the spiritual strength to listen rather than to judge, to seek peace even when it eludes us time and again. Thereby shall we be your children. Amen.

Samuel
Changing Times

*The people refused to listen to Samuel.
"No!" they said. "We want a king over
us. Then we will be like all the other
nations, with a king to lead us and to
go out before us and fight our battles."
(1 Sam 8:19-20, NIV)*

Samuel was the last and best of the judges. Faithful and focused, he never had a prodigal season. He did not live a lazy life. At retirement age, he deserved to have an airport or an interstate highway named after him. But the people wanted no more judges. They wanted a king like other nations, one who would fight their battles for them. What a naïve request!

Samuel's first response was to ask the Lord, and the Lord agreed with Samuel: the people were actually rejecting the Lord himself. Nevertheless, God instructed Samuel to listen to the people. So Samuel continued in the spirit of a servant in a dawning new age.

Samuel was the transition from judges to kings. He anointed Israel's first two kings, Saul and David. It was a terribly awkward, unbalanced time for the Hebrew nation—stuck between a dying model of judges and a new model of kings not yet birthed. Yet God through Samuel laid the foundations for Israel's most glorious days under David and his son Solomon, just one generation away.

Changing times are awkward and unbalanced for nearly everybody, but particularly for those of us whom God calls to be the transition people: appreciating the past but leading into a future that we do not fully understand. Looking at Samuel's story helps us cope with our anxiety overload in changing times. He was indeed treated unfairly and disrespectfully. Even so, he was able not to gratify his own wishes except the wish to serve the Lord and the people.

Those are good attitudinal footsteps to follow in our changing times with family, friends, and acquaintances.

A Quote to Remember

It is not the strongest of the species that survive, nor the most intelligent, but the one most responsive to change.[122] (Author unknown)

Think on These Things

I the LORD do not change. (Mal 3:6, NIV)

Do not be anxious about anything, but in everything by prayer and supplication with thanksgiving let your requests be made known to God. And the peace of God, which surpasses all understanding, will guard your hearts and your minds in Christ Jesus. (Phil 4:6-7, ESV)

By faith Abraham obeyed when he was called to go out to a place that he was to receive as an inheritance. And he went out, not knowing where he was going. (Heb 11:8, ESV)

Prayer

Lord, I'm not all that comfortable with the way the world is changing. Please help me understand how to be a help and not a hindrance to your plans for tomorrow. Amen.

95 **Saul**
Jealousy, the Green-eyed Monster

*Saul, a choice and handsome man,
and there was not a more handsome
person than he among the sons of
Israel; from his shoulders and up he
was taller than any of the people.
(1 Sam 9:2, NASB)*

Naïve and popular misconceptions often put incompetent people in authority in business, politics, religion, and elsewhere. The Hebrews' naïve wish for a king to fight their battles for them (1 Sam 8:19-20) made Saul their obvious choice; he looked the part. But he was neither an administrator nor a spiritual leader. He seems not even to have had a normal soldier's courage in the incident with the giant Philistine, Goliath (1 Sam 17). Whether it was the cause or a symptom of a deeper cause, the most obvious scriptural explanation for Saul's demise was his insane jealousy of David, beginning when David killed Goliath.

A spiritual person might have taken his jealous tendencies to the Lord and managed or eradicated them. A godly administrator might have perceived that overcoming his personal jealousy had to be first priority for the sake of giving good leadership to the kingdom. A normally courageous soldier might have had at least the emotional strength to prevent his jealousy from destroying his mental health. But Saul was none of these. Jealousy joined to his other inabilities made his downfall a certainty.

It's painful to see someone accomplish what we did not accomplish. It's discouraging to hear people praise someone else more than they praise us. That pain and discouragement, however, should call our attention to the deadly, creeping malignancy of unchecked jealousy. The easiest and most effective time to take the high road is when jealousy first sets foot in our hearts. At any time, the cost of reigning it in is far less than the cost of allowing it to continue.

Today is the best of times to take our jealousy to the Great Physician and find a cure.

A Quote to Remember

Beware . . . of jealousy . . . the green-eyed monster.[123] (William Shakespeare)

Think on These Things

[Saul] said, "They credit David with ten thousands and me with only thousands. Next they'll be making him their king!" So Saul kept a jealous eye on David. (1 Sam 18:8-9, NLT)

Anger is cruel, and wrath is like a flood, but jealousy is even more dangerous. (Prov 27:4, NLT)

The LORD's arm is not too weak to save you. It's your sins that have cut you off from God. Because of your sins, he has turned away and will not listen anymore. (Isa 59:1-2, NLT)

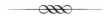

Prayer

Lord, keep me free of the web of jealousy, I pray. Fill my heart with virtues and my hands with deeds that leave no room for evil feelings like jealousy. Amen.

96 **Solomon**
Good Start, Bad Finish

So Solomon did evil in the eyes of the LORD; he did not follow the LORD completely, as David his father had done. (1 Kgs 11:6, NIV)

Athletic stamina to the end of the contest is a great thing. Spiritual stamina to the end of our lives is also a great thing. Solomon is known for his wise prayer at the beginning of his kingship, his wisdom as a ruler, the magnificent temple he built, and for taking Israel to its highest status ever among the nations.

There are signs, however, that his later years were not as praiseworthy. That's an ugly fact worded nicely. Solomon's spiritual stamina declined greatly. His magnificent building program was accomplished by "forced labor" (1 Kings 5:13, 9:15, NIV). His godly character eroded in tragic proportions.

First Kings 11 tells of Solomon's further spiritual decline: loving many foreign women, building shrines to other gods, worshiping those gods himself. God even declared that, for the sake of David, the kingdom would remain united as long as Solomon, David's son, lived, but thereafter it would be torn apart. And indeed it was torn apart within months of Solomon's death.

This kind of good start, bad finish story happens frequently enough to merit attention. It is a warning to the wise. If the man often spoken of as "the wisest man who ever lived" could fall so far and so badly, surely none of us can consider ourselves beyond the realm of that possibility.

Let us then redouble our resolve that the passing years will find us drawing closer to the Lord rather than falling away;

not abandoning the good decisions made in younger years but rather building on the best of our youth; not regressing to the worship of other gods but rather growing in spirituality.

A Quote to Remember

Nobody grows old merely by living a number of years. We grow old by deserting our ideals.[124] (Samuel Ullman)

Think on These Things

However, I consider my life worth nothing to me; my only aim is to finish the race and complete the task the Lord Jesus has given me. (Acts 20:24, NIV)

I have fought the good fight, I have finished the race, I have kept the faith. (2 Tim 4:7, NIV)

So let us stop going over the basic teachings about Christ again and again. Let us go on instead and become mature in our understanding. Surely we don't need to start again with the fundamental importance of repenting from evil deeds and placing our faith in God. (Heb 6:1, NLT)

Prayer

God, I pray for strength to increase in faithfulness as time goes by. Build determination and perseverance in me. Send encouragements and motivations. Help me finish strong. In Jesus' name, amen.

97 **The Sower**
A Bountiful Harvest Guaranteed

But other seeds fell on good soil and produced a crop, some a hundred, some sixty, and some thirty times what was sown. (Matt 13:8, ISV)

This parable is our Lord's promise that there will most assuredly be good results when we serve at his direction. Start a Bible study, lead a group, befriend someone who seems alone. God's power transforms, multiplies, and rewards our work for him.

Modern cultivation methods and fertilizers have multiplied crop yields many times over anything that was possible in Jesus' day. Reaping thirty times the amount of seed that was sown would be a good harvest. A hundredfold harvest was unheard of. Jesus was warning his disciples that some of their efforts would be fruitless, like seed that falls on hard ground. Nevertheless, all things considered, there would be a huge harvest.

In this same chapter, he teaches that the kingdom of God grows tremendously like mustard seed, expands dramatically like yeast, is worth everything like a great treasure or the finest pearl. He's encouraging first-century and twenty-first-century disciples to sow the gospel seed in whatever way available to us because that seed is powerful.

He spoke about a sower who spreads many seeds in a sweeping motion. He was not speaking about planting each seed in a carefully chosen spot. That means that we are to sow the gospel seed indiscriminately, wherever there is opportunity. We cannot know which seeds will sprout and thrive. We cannot know whether the rains will favor the high ground or the low.

But the God of the rains knows, and he promises a fantastic harvest if we sow the seed.

A Quote to Remember

Keep on sowing your seed, for you never know which will grow; perhaps it all will.[125] (Albert Einstein)

Think on These Things

Those who plant in tears will harvest with shouts of joy. They weep as they go to plant their seed, but they sing as they return with the harvest. (Ps 126:5-6, NLT)

He said to his disciples, "The harvest is great, but the workers are few." (Matt 9:37, NLT)

Do not be deceived: God cannot be mocked. A man reaps what he sows. Whoever sows to please their flesh, from the flesh will reap destruction; whoever sows to please the Spirit, from the Spirit will reap eternal life. Let us not become weary in doing good, for at the proper time we will reap a harvest if we do not give up. (Gal 6:7-9, NIV)

Prayer

God of seed, God of soil, bless the sowing we pray. Send the rain; send the sun; bless the growing we pray. Multiply our faith; multiply our work for a bountiful harvest. Amen.

98 Stephen
Called by a Problem

They chose Stephen, a man full of faith and of the Holy Spirit. (Acts 6:5, NIV)

We often rise to our best selves because of a problem. The church in Jerusalem had a food distribution program, and some Greek-speaking Christians complained that their widows were receiving less than the Hebrew-speaking widows. This problem occasioned the selection of the seven, whom we have identified as the first deacons, to oversee the distribution. Stephen was the first named, meaning that he was the most favored or the most outstanding.

He and the other six must have had administrative ability to distribute the food fairly, and also relationship abilities to resolve the complaining. Many would-be leaders are strong in administration or in relationships, but not in both. Good leadership and peacemaking has to balance the two.

Families are held together by those who balance Stephen's two abilities effectively. Group friendships are maintained through the years by abilities gained when a problem arose and someone stepped up to become a better person in order to resolve the situation. That's one of the ways God works all things together for the good of those who love him (Rom 8:28).

We have frequent opportunities to step up to our better selves when a problem or a hurdle of some kind looms in our path. Some live by the adage, "when the going gets tough, the smart get lost." Stephen and the other six first deacons had a much better idea.

A Quote to Remember

The dogmas of the quiet past are inadequate to the stormy present. The occasion is piled high with difficulty, and we must rise with the occasion. As our case is new, so we must think anew and act anew.[126] (Abraham Lincoln)

Think on These Things

Then Caleb silenced the people before Moses and said, "We should go up and take possession of the land, for we can certainly do it." But the men who had gone up with him said, "We can't attack those people; they are stronger than we are. We seemed like grasshoppers in our own eyes, and we looked the same to them." (Num 13:30-31, 33, NIV)

David said, "The LORD who delivered me from the paw of the lion and from the paw of the bear, He will deliver me from the hand of this Philistine." (1 Sam 17:37, NASB)

Strive for peace with everyone, and for the holiness without which no one will see the Lord. See to it that no one fails to obtain the grace of God; that no "root of bitterness" springs up and causes trouble, and by it many become defiled. (Heb 12:14-15, ESV)

Prayer

Lord, bless the peacemakers, those with courage and grace to calm troubled waters. And make me one of them I pray. In Jesus' name, amen.

99 The Wise Men
Disappearing Worshipers

Where is the one who has been born king of the Jews? We saw his star when it rose and have come to worship him. (Matt 2:2, NIV)

The wise men (also called kings or magi) bring a bright element to our Christmas pageants and also to our understanding of Jesus as Lord of all nations. We rightly draw inspiration from their presence at the manger.

But why do they disappear altogether? Are they in fact good examples of those who come to the Lord for a brief moment and then go on about their lives as before: worshipers who seem to be the real thing but who disappear quickly? They are not mentioned in the rest of the New Testament. Some believe they became Christians, but the church has questioned that.

They may have been much like the people Paul encountered in Athens who "spend their time in nothing other than telling or hearing something new" (Acts 17:21, NASB). Our God calls us to be more than tasters of faith and experimenters in religion. There are those who try first one thing and then another, and never settle down to faith that dominates their lives.

The picture that is accurate to the truth shows these three men bowing before Jesus, bringing to him the best gifts they had. Gold, the prince of metals, was a gift fit for a king. Frankincense, perfume used in anointing, was a gift fit for a priest. Myrrh, used in embalming, was an appropriate gift for one who was to die. The Bethlehem baby was indeed our King and Priest, who came to die. We also should bring to him the best that we have.

A Quote to Remember

Worship is giving God the best that He has given you. Be careful what you do with the best you have. Whenever you get a blessing from God, give it back to Him as a love gift.[127] (Oswald Chambers)

Think on These Things

Come, let us worship and bow down. Let us kneel before the LORD our Maker. (Ps 95:6, NASB)

Worship the LORD in the splendor of his holiness; tremble before him, all the earth. (Ps 96:9, NIV)

Therefore God exalted him to the highest place and gave him the name that is above every name, that at the name of Jesus every knee should bow, in heaven and on earth and under the earth, and every tongue acknowledge that Jesus Christ is Lord. (Phil 2:9-11, NIV)

Prayer

Heavenly Father, I've noticed those who taste religion, keeping you and your church at arm's length, and I want to live closer to you than that. You are indeed for me the King of kings and Lord of lords. I bow my heart and soul before you in worship, now and always. Amen.

100 Zacchaeus
Trying to See Jesus

When Jesus came by, he looked up at Zacchaeus and called him by name. "Zacchaeus!" he said. "Quick, come down! I must be a guest in your home today." (Luke 19:5, NLT)

When we seek the Lord, he comes more than halfway, as we see in Zacchaeus's experience. This is a strange and touching picture: a man old enough to have grown wealthy, short of stature, climbing a tree to see a popular rabbi. Why did he do that?

Hated people, and especially short hated people, are not fond of crowds. People don't smile or even look at you. If the crowd is pressed close together, some take joy in obstructing your vision and blocking your way. Zacchaeus knew constant ostracism to the point that getting close to Jesus in that crowd was an unpleasant task if not completely impossible.

Zacchaeus had some real interest in seeing Jesus. It's possible that he was just curious, but that's unlikely for a wealthy man climbing a tree. It's more probable that Zacchaeus had significant religious convictions, but he was shut out from the temple and from normal religious events. He was eager to hear, but nobody would share with him. He was open to godly faith, but the guardians at religion's door judged him unworthy. Perhaps he had heard Jesus teach that those who seek are the ones who find (Luke 11:9). He came to the sycamore seeking the Lord, and found him.

Zacchaeus's response to Jesus indicates that some foundation had been laid in his heart and mind before that day.

Some people are impetuous enough to make important decisions on the spur of the moment, and surely the Lord can bring about that kind of response if he chooses. But in all probability, Zacchaeus had a ready heart. From somewhere in his experience, God's Holy Spirit had been preparing him for that day, for that moment.

God prepares us in advance too for our meeting with him. Perhaps today.

A Quote to Remember

Take one step toward God, and he'll take a thousand steps toward you.[128] (Author unknown)

Think on These Things

If you look for me wholeheartedly, you will find me. (Jer 29:13, NLT)

Come close to God, and God will come close to you. (Jas 4:8, NLT)

I love all who love me. Those who search will surely find me. (Prov 8:17, NLT)

Prayer

Father God, I love you and I want to love you more. I want to seek you more wholeheartedly. I know that I get too preoccupied with my own agenda, and most of the times when I seek you, I'm just wanting you to help me in what I've decided to do. Forgive me. Grant me Zacchaeus's spirit of seeking you and his willingness to receive you into his home and heart as Lord and master. Amen.

Notes

1. C. S. Lewis, *Mere Christianity*, quoted in "Quotes about Christ," www.goodreads.com/quotes/tag/christ (accessed 9 October 2013).

2. Pope John Paul II, Homily in a Holy Mass at the Capital Mall, Washington DC, 7 October 1979, www.vatican.va/holy_father/ john_paul_ii/homilies/1979/documents/hf_jp-ii_hom_19791007_ usa-washington_en.html (accessed 9 October 2013).

3. Adapted from a prayer by Joe A. Lieway, in "A Servant's Prayer," *A Time for God*, slu.edu/prayerbook/2010/08/14/a-servants-prayer/ (accessed 9 October 2013).

4. Billy Graham, "Say What?" Church of the Brethren. www.brethren. org/stewardship/documents/stewardship-quotes.pdf (accessed 10 October 2013).

5. Roy McClain, *If with All Your Heart* (Westwood NJ: Revell Co., 1961) 105.

6. Cindy Gerard, in *To the Limit*, quoted in "Quotes about Growing Up," www.goodreads.com/quotes/tag/growing-up?page=2 (accessed 12 October 2013) (this quote also attributed to Chili Davis, major league baseball player and coach).

7. Attributed without documentation to Mahatma Gandhi.

8. William Wordsworth, from "Lines Composed a Few Miles above Tintern Abbey," stanza 11, *On Revisiting the Banks of the Wye During a Tour*, 13 July 1798.

9. "For My Friends," Prayer for Your Neighbor category of *Your Catholic Guide*, www.yourcatholicguide.com/prayers-and-devotions/your-neighbor/for-my-friends.html (accessed 26 September 2013).

10. Autolycus in William Shakespeare, *Winter's Tale*," act 4, scene 3, found at *The Complete Works of William Shakespeare*, shakespeare.mit.edu/ winters_tale/full.html (accessed 28 September 2013).

11. Billy Graham, *Peace with God* (Nashville: W. Publishing Group, 2002) ch. 19, "Peace at Last," p. 219; found at www.gotothebible.com/HTML/peacewithGod19.html (accessed 28 September 2013).

12. Edward G. Bulwer-Lytton, quoted in *God's Treasury of Virtues* (Tulsa OK: Honor Books, 1995) 171.

13. Sophocles, found at *Inspire the Planet*, www.inspiretheplanet.com/inspirational-quotes/sophocles-kindness-quote/ (29 September 2013).

14. Mahatma Gandhi, found at "Action," *Living Life Fully*, www.livinglifefully.com/action.html (accessed 29 September 2013).

15. Morning Prayer, Prayer Archive of World Prayers, found at www.worldprayers.org/archive/prayers/invocations/o_infinite_god_of_life.html (accessed 29 September 2013).

16. Jessica Harris, "Faithful, not Successful," *Catholic Womanhood*, found at Catholic News Agency, www.catholicnewsagency.com/cw/post.php?id=564 (accessed 29 September 2013).

17. Elbert Hubbard, in *The Notebook*, izquotes.com/quote/321262 (accessed 31 August 2015).

18. Leonardo da Vinci, in *How God Sees You*, found at The Cove, Leonardo da Vinci Quotes, www.miniwebtool.com/quote-search/by-author/?author=Leonardo%20da%20Vinci (accessed 30 September 2013).

19. Max Lucado, in *When God Whispers Your Name* (Dallas: Word Publishing, 1994); found at maxlucado.com/read/excerpts/when-god-whispers-your-name/ (accessed 2 September 2013).

20. J. C. Ryle, Assurance Quotes, found at Christian Quotes, christian-quotes.ochristian.com/Assurance-Quotes/page-2.shtml (accessed 4 November 2013).

21. Arthur Jersild, Quotes on Compassion, found at Center for Building a Culture of Empathy, cultureofempathy.com/References/Quotes/Compassion.htm (1 October 2013).

22. Nathaniel Branden, https://www.randomactsofkindness.org/inspirational-kindness-quotes/3145-there-is-overwhelming-evidence-that-the-higher-the-level-of (accessed 31 August 2015).

23. Nathaniel Branden and Anna Freud, Inspiring Quotations, found at Values.Com, www.values.com/inspirational-quotes/value/81-Confidence (2 October 2013).

24. Alexander Hamilton, Quotes about Discretion, found at Goodreads, www.goodreads.com/quotes/tag/discretion (6 February 2014).

25. Henri Frederic Amiel, Discretion Quotes, found at Thinkexist. com, thinkexist.com/quotes/with/keyword/discretion/2.html (6 February 2014).

26. Jean de La Fontaine, Discretion Quotes, found at Brainy Quote, www.brainyquote.com/quotes/keywords/discretion.html (6 February 2014).

27. R. L. Sharpe, "A Bag of Tools," found at FaithForward.org, faith-forward.org/isn-t-it-strange-.htm (2 October 2013).

28. George Herbert, Quotations Book, found at quotationsbook.com/ quote/15517/#sthash.vKba7Q8T.dpbs (3 October 2013).

29. Author unknown, "Watch Our Words, Inc.," at watchourwords. org/ (3 October 2013).

30. Rossiter Worthington Raymond, 1840-1918, NetHymnal, cyber-hymnal.org/bio/r/a/raymond_rw.htm (5 November 2013).

31. Tad Williams, Quotations about Honesty, found at *The Quote Garden*, www.quotegarden.com/honesty.html (accessed 3 October 2013).

32. Emily Dickinson, "Hope is the Thing with Feathers," found at *Poetry Foundation*, www.poetryfoundation.org/poem/171619 (accessed 8 November 2013).

33. Anne Lamott, Quotations about Hope, found at *The Quote Garden*, www.quotegarden.com/hope.html (accessed 4 October 2013).

34. Charles L. Allen, Quotations about Hope, found at *The Quote Garden*, www.quotegarden.com/hope.html (accessed 4 October 2013).

35. Martin Luther King, Jr., *A Call to Conscience* (New York: IPM in association with Warner Books, 2001) 158.

36. Socrates, found at *The Quotations Page*, www.quotationspage.com/quote/2871.html (accessed 8 November 2013).

37. Benjamin Disraeli, found at *SearchQuotes*, www.search-quotes.com/quotation/The_legacy_of_heroes_is_the_memory_of_a_great_name_and_the_inheritance_of_a_great_example./224666/ (accessed 8 November 2013).

38. Henry David Thoreau, found at *Quotations Book*, quotationsbook.com/quote/6911/#sthash.0UfdaMkL.dpbs (accessed 8 November 2013).

39. Martin Luther King, Jr., speech, St. Louis MO, 22 March 1964, found at Martin Luther King Jr. Quotes, About.com, history1900s.about.com/od/martinlutherkingjr/a/mlkquotes.htm (accessed 4 October 2013).

40. Robert Louis Stevenson, found at *The Happiness Project* www.happiness-project.com/happiness_project/2012/02/quiet-minds-cannot-be-perplexed-or-frightened/ (accessed 4 October 2013).

41. John Milton, found at Values.com, www.values.com/inspirational-quotes/5490-Gratitude-Bestows-Reverence- (accessed 5 October 2013).

42. William Barclay, "The Lovely Things," in *The Letters to the Galatians and Ephesians*, Daily Study Bible Series (Philadelphia: The Westminster Press, 1958) 54, 57.

43. William Paul Young, author of *The Shack*, found at Quotes about Submission, www.goodreads.com/quotes/tag/submission (accessed 8 October 2013).

44. J. Winston Pearce, *To Brighten Each Day* (Nashville: Broadman Press, 1983) 308.

45. Dale Carnegie, *Dale Carnegie's Scrapbook* (New York: Simon and Schuster, 1959) 98, 102.

46. Aristotle, found at *Quotations Book*, quotationsbook.com/quote/15930/#sthash.T14any0h.dpbs (accessed 11 November 2013).

47. Attributed to Calvin Coolidge, found at www.goodreads.com/quotes/tag/judgmental (accessed 9 October 2013).

48. Toba Beta in "My Ancestor Was an Ancient Astronaut," found at www.goodreads.com/quotes/tag/judgmental (accessed 9 October 2013).

49. Mohandas Karamchand Gandhi, found at *Living Life Fully*, www.livinglifefully.com/thinkersmgandhi.html (accessed 2 November 2013).

50. Aristotle, found at "Achieve College Success," www.achievecollege-success.com/blog/?tag=vocation (accessed 12 October 2013).

51. Martin Luther King, Jr., found at *MLK Day*, mlkday.gov/plan/library/communications/quotes.php (accessed 13 November 2013).

52. Napoleon Bonaparte, found at SharperThink, sharperthink.word-press.com/2011/08/14/a-leader-is-a-dealer-in-hope/ (accessed 12 October 2013).

53. Ralph Waldo Emerson on recognizing greatness in others, found at Joya Martin, www.joyamartin.com/ralph-waldo-emerson/ (accessed 12 October 2013).

54. Jim Gallery, New Life Daily Devotion, found at *Crosswalk. com*, www.crosswalk.com/devotionals/newlife/new-life-daily-devotion-october-31-2011.html (accessed 13 October 2013).

55. From "Make Me a Blessing," Ira B. Wilson, SCHULER, www.hymnary.org/text/out_in_the_highways_and_by_ways_of_life (accessed 13 October 2013).

56. Jacqueline A. Moore, *Moments of My Life* (Fort Valley VA: Loft Press, 1999) 61.

57. Adapted from Adoniram Judson, found at www.whatchristian-swanttoknow.com/20-bible-verses-to-comfort-the-hurting/ (4 November 2013).

58. Adapted from George Dawson's Prayer of Comfort, found at www.beliefnet.com/Faiths/Faith-Tools/Meditation/2005/01/Prayers-Of-Comfort-And-Hope.aspx.

59. Barack Obama, quoted in David Maraniss, "The College Years," *The Guardian*, www.guardian.co.uk/world/2012/may/25/barack-obama-the-college-years#start-of-comments (7 September 2012).

60. Adapted from Chauncey Spencer's Prayer for Brotherhood, found at www.lwfaah.net/prayer.htm (accessed 1 September 2013).

61. Dale Carnegie, *Dale Carnegie's Scrapbook* (New York: Simon & Schuster, 1959) 159.

62. Ralph Waldo Emerson, found at intentionomics.com/articles/purpose-life (accessed 16 October 2013).

63. Peter S. Beagle, from *The Last Unicorn*, found at www.inspirationalstories.com/quotes/t/peter-s-beagle-s-book-the-last-unicorn/page/2/ (accessed 16 October 2013).

64. Martin Luther King, Jr., "I Have a Dream" speech, 28 August 1963, Lincoln Memorial, in Washington DC, found in the National Archives, www.archives.gov/press/exhibits/dream-speech.pdf (accessed 17 October 2013).

65. "Undivided Heart," words by Dennis Lewallen, Broadman Press, Nashville, 1999.

66. Charles Spurgeon, "An Undivided Heart," solumevangelium.wordpress.com/2010/04/17/an-undivided-heart/ (accessed 3 November 2013).

67. Henry Wadsworth Longfellow, from chapter 8 of *Hyperion*, found at the Literature Network, www.online-literature.com/henry_longfellow/hyperion/35/ (accessed 17 October 2013).

68. Dodie Smith, "Increase Happiness Through Noble Deeds and Hot Baths," found at *Make the Change*, makethechange.com.au/increase-happiness-through-noble-deeds-and-hot-baths/ (6 November 2013).

69. Charles Stanley, *Inspirational Quotes on Prayer*, www.thoughts-about-god.com/quotes/quotes-prayer.htm (accessed 2 November 2013).

70. Caryll Houselander "The Value of Sin," myemail.constantcontact.com/Daily-Devotion.html?soid=1106306412045&aid=oDCeosY-GYo (accessed 18 October 2013).

71. William Paul Young, "The Value of Sin," myemail.constantcontact.com/Daily-Devotion.html?soid=1106306412045&aid=oDCeosY-GYo (accessed 18 October 2013).

72. W. Clement Stone, in *What Will Matter* by Michael Josephson, whatwillmatter.com/2013/05/quote-poster-have-the-courage-to-say-no-have-the-courage-to-face-the-truth-do-the-right-thing-because-it-is-right-these-are-the-magic-keys-to-living-your-life-with-integrity-w-clement-stone/ (accessed 18 October 2013).

73. Aristotle, found at www.goodreads.com/author/quotes/2192. Aristotle (accessed 18 October 2013).

74. Adapted from A Prayer for Peacemaking, found at *Catholic Online*, www.catholic.org/prayers/prayer.php?p=1614 (accessed 19 October 2013).

75. Margaret Mead, from *The World Ahead: An Anthropologist Anticipates the Future*, quoted at www.goodreads.com/quotes/137186-never-believe-that-a-few-caring-people-can-t-change-the (accessed 19 October 2013).

76. Richard Whately, found at www.winwisdom.com/quotes/topic/selfishness.aspx (accessed 19 October 2013).

77. James Russell Lowell, "The Present Crisis," found at *Poets.org*, www.poets.org/viewmedia.php/prmMID/19385 (accessed 2 November 2013).

78. William Hazlitt, found at *thoughtjoy.com*, www.thoughtjoy.com/william-hazlitt/we-grow-tired-of-everything-but-turning-others-into-ridicule (accessed 20 October 2013).

79. Tacitus, "28. The Murder Of Galba," in *The Histories by Cornelius Tacitus*, A Theory of Civilization, www.ourcivilisation.com/smartboard/shop/tacitusc/histries/chap2.htm (accessed 20 October 2013).

80. Karl Pillemer, "Long-Term Effects of Favoritism," *Metro Parent*, www.metroparent.com/Metro-Parent/February-2011/Long-Term-Effects-of-Favoritism/ (accessed 20 October 2013).

81. Fyodor Dostoyevsky, in *The Brothers Karamazov*, found at nathanrosenblumjustice, nathanrosenblumjustice.wordpress.com/2012/04/19/fyodor-dostoevsky/ (accessed 21 October 2013).

82. Christos Yannaras, Variation on the Song of Songs, www.goodreads. com/work/quotes/4474975-variations-on-the-song-of-songs (accessed 31 August 2015).

83. Mother Teresa, found at *Positively Positive*, www.positivelypositive. com/quotes/yesterday-is-gone-tomorrow-has-not-yet-come-we-have-only-today-let-us-begin/ (21 October 2013).

84. Mahatma Gandhi, BBC World Service, www.bbc.co.uk/ worldservice/learningenglish/movingwords/shortlist/gandhi.shtml (accessed 21 October 2013).

85. Helen Keller, found at *Tentmaker*, www.tentmaker.org/Quotes/ sufferingquotes.htm (accessed 25 October 2013).

86. Adapted from "Prayer of Resignation in Suffering," *Prayers in Time of Suffering*, http://rcp.wikia.com/wiki/Prayer_of_Resignation_in_ Suffering (accessed 16 September 2015).

87. Glenda Green, found at *Spiritual Transformation*, www. spiritual-transformation.net/Quotes/ (accessed 25 October 2013).

88. Eddie Espinosa, "Change My Heart O God," www.hymnary.org/ text/change_my_heart_o_god (accessed 25 October 2013).

89. Edmund Burke, found at www.leadershipnow.com/humility-quotes.html (accessed 25 October 2013).

90. Adapted from a prayer by William Barclay, found at *Ram's Horn Studio*, www.ramshornstudio.com/humility.htm (accessed 25 October 2013).

91. Arabian Proverb, in "How to Become a Magnet for Friends: 7 Mindful Tips," found at tinybuddha.com/blog/how-to-become-a-magnet-for-friends-7-mindful-tips/ (accessed 7 November 2013).

92. Adapted from Martin Luther King, Jr., found at www.blfnvcenter. com/Building_Life_Foundations_Nonviolence_Center/Welcome.html (accessed 25 October 2013).

93. Ralph Waldo Emerson, essay 3: "Compensation," found at classiclit.about.com/library/bl-etexts/rwemerson/bl-rwemer-essays-3.htm (accessed 25 October 2013).

94. A Prayer for Integrity, *A Daily Prayer*, adailyprayer.wordpress. com/2008/02/27/a-prayer-for-integrity/ (accessed 25 October 2013).

95. Oswald Chambers, quoted at www.goodreads.com/author/ quotes/41469.Oswald_Chambers (accessed 25 October 2013).

96. Adapted from Thomas Merton's prayer, from "Thoughts in Solitude," found at www.goodreads.com/quotes/80913-my-Lord-god-i-have-no-idea-where-i-am (accessed 25 October 2013).

97. Bryant McGill, found at www.quotes.net/quotations/control%20 freak (accessed 26 October 2013).

98. Mother Teresa, found at www.quotesvalley.com/loneliness-and-the-feeling-of-being-unwanted-is-the-most-terrible-poverty-2/ (accessed 26 October 2013).

99. Stephen King, found at www.brainyquote.com/quotes/keywords/ devil_5.html (accessed 26 October 2013).

100. Harry Segall, found at www.brainyquote.com/quotes/keywords/ devil_5.html (accessed 26 October 2013).

101. William Barclay, *The Letters to the Corinthians*, Daily Bible Study (Philadelphia: The Westminster Press, 1956) 120.

102. C. S. Lewis, quoted in Kristen L. McNulty, "The Art of Friendship," for The Mad Christian Radio Show, www.madradioshow.net/ impact/impactart.html (accessed 26 October 2013).

103. Denis Parsons Burkitt, found at thinkexist.com/quotes/with/ keyword/pondering/ (accessed 27 October 2013).

104. Turkish Proverb, found at thinkexist.com/quotes/with/keyword/ pondering/ (accessed 27 October 2013).

105. Adlai E. Stevenson, found at www.searchquotes.com/quotes/ about/Prejudice/3/ (accessed 27 October 2013).

106. Henry David Thoreau, found at www.searchquotes.com/quotes/ about/Prejudice/3/ (accessed 27 October 2013).

107. "7 Quotes to Inspire you to Keep Learning," Huffpost Home, www.huffingtonpost.com/2013/09/03/education-quotes-learning-quotes_n_3830956.html#slide=2859760 (accessed 27 October 2013).

108. Adapted from Prayers for Spiritual Growth, *Chosen One Ministries*, chosenoneministries.com/PRAYERS/prayers_for_spiritual_growth.htm (accessed 27 October 2013).

109. Ekhart Tolle, found at www.spiritual-transformation.net/Quotes/ (accessed 28 October 2013).

110. Adapted from John Henry Cardinal Newman, Prayer for Christlikeness, www.loyolapress.com/prayer-for-christlikeness-cardinal-newman.htm (accessed 28 October 2013).

111. Jonathan Edwards, found at www.goodreads.com/quotes/tag/holiness (accessed 28 October 2013).

112. Various versions of this quote are attributed to several authors; among them are Robert Louis Stevenson and Mother Teresa.

113. A. W. Tozer, found at christian-quotes.ochristian.com/Surrender-Quotes (accessed 28 October 2013).

114. Maimonides, found at www.brainyquote.com/quotes/keywords/indecision.html (accessed 28 October 2013).

115. Adapted from Prayer Before an Important Decision, Ithaca College, www.ithaca.edu/sacl/catholic/prayers/decision/ (accessed 28 October 2013).

116. Adapted from Søren Kierkegaard, found at dailychristianquote.com/dcqprodigal.html (accessed 29 October 2013).

117. Opening lyrics to a popular American song in the late twentieth century that was sung by Elvis, Johnny Cash, and others.

118. Dante Alighieri, found at web.stagram.com/p/170777945_353535 (accessed 29 October 2013).

119. From a popular Christian children's song in the mid-1900s.

120. Adapted from An All-Inclusive Prayer, Adoration Lutheran Church, adorationlc.org/2012/01/25/an-all-inclusive-prayer-for-lent-2012/.

121. Francis Bacon, found at www.giga-usa.com/quotes/topics/ revenge_t001.htm (accessed 29 October 2013).

122. Author unknown, commonly misattributed to Charles Darwin, found at www.quotegarden.com/change.html (accessed 30 October 2013).

123. William Shakespeare, *Othello*, 3.3, shakespeare.mit.edu/othello/ full.html (accessed 30 October 2013).

124. Samuel Ullman, found at www.uab.edu/ullmanmuseum/ (accessed 30 October 2013).

125. Albert Einstein, found at *The Gathering Place*, thegatheringplace-home.myfastforum.org/archive/may-20-2013-seeds__o_t__t_2175.html (accessed 30 October 2013).

126. From Abraham Lincoln's annual message to Congress, 1 December 1862, Speeches and Writings, Abraham Lincoln online, www.abraham-lincolnonline.org/lincoln/speeches/congress.htm (accessed 1 November 2013).

127. Oswald Chambers, found at deeperchristianquotes.com/page/2 (accessed 1 November 2013).

128. Author unknown. There are numerous and varied versions of this quote.

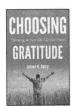

Crossroads in Christian Growth
W. Loyd Allen

Authentic Christian life presents spiritual crises and we struggle to find a hero walking with God at a crossroads. With wisdom and sincerity, W. Loyd Allen presents Jesus as our example and these crises as stages in the journey of growth we each take toward maturity in Christ. *978-1-57312-753-0 164 pages/pb* **$15.00**

A Divine Duet
Ministry and Motherhood
Alicia Davis Porterfield, ed.

Each essay in this inspiring collection is as different as the mother-minister who wrote it, from theologians to chaplains, inner-city ministers to rural-poverty ministers, youth pastors to preachers, mothers who have adopted, birthed, and done both. *978-1-57312-676-2 146 pages/pb* **$16.00**

The Exile and Beyond (All the Bible series)
Wayne Ballard

The Exile and Beyond brings to life the sacred literature of Israel and Judah that comprises the exilic and postexilic communities of faith. It covers Ezekiel, Isaiah, Haggai, Zechariah, Malachi, 1 & 2 Chronicles, Ezra, Nehemiah, Joel, Jonah, Song of Songs, Esther, and Daniel. *978-1-57312-759-2 196 pages/pb* **$16.00**

Ezekiel (Smyth & Helwys Annual Bible Study series)
God's Presence in Performance
William D. Shiell

Through a four-session Bible study for individuals and groups, Shiell interprets the book of Ezekiel as a four-act drama to be told to those living out their faith in a strange, new place. Shiell encourages congregations to listen to God's call, accept where God has planted them, surrender the shame of their past, receive a new heart from God, and allow God to breathe new life into them. *Teaching Guide 978-1-57312-755-4 192 pages/pb* **$14.00**
Study Guide 978-1-57312-756-1 126 pages/pb **$6.00**

Fierce Love
Desperate Measures for Desperate Times
Jeanie Miley

Fierce Love is about learning to see yourself and know yourself as a conduit of love, operating from a full heart instead of trying to find someone to whom you can hook up your emotional hose and fill up your empty heart. *978-1-57312-810-0 276 pages/pb* **$18.00**

Five Hundred Miles
Reflections on Calling and Pilgrimage
Lauren Brewer Bass

Spain's Camino de Santiago, the Way of St. James, has been a cherished pilgrimage path for centuries, visited by countless people searching for healing, solace, purpose, and hope. These stories from her five-hundred-mile-walk is Lauren Brewer Bass's honest look at the often winding, always surprising journey of a calling. *978-1-57312-812-4 142 pages/pb* **$16.00**

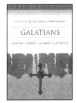

Galatians (Smyth & Helwys Bible Commentary)
Marion L. Soards and Darrell J. Pursiful

In Galatians, Paul endeavored to prevent the Gentile converts from embracing a version of the gospel that insisted on their observance of a form of the Mosaic Law. He saw with a unique clarity that such a message reduced the crucified Christ to being a mere agent of the Law. For Paul, the gospel of Jesus Christ alone, and him crucified, had no place in it for the claim that Law-observance was necessary for believers to experience the power of God's grace. *978-1-57312-771-4 384 pages/hc* **$55.00**

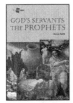

God's Servants the Prophets
Bryan Bibb

God's Servants, the Prophets covers the Israelite and Judean prophetic literature from the preexilic period. It includes Amos, Hosea, Isaiah, Micah, Zephaniah, Nahum, Habakkuk, Jeremiah, and Obadiah. *978-1-57312-758-5 208 pages/pb* **$16.00**

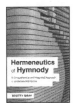

Hermeneutics of Hymnody
A Comprehensive and Integrated Approach to Understanding Hymns
Scotty Gray

Scotty Gray's *Hermeneutics of Hymnody* is a comprehensive and integrated approach to understanding hymns. It is unique in its holistic and interrelated exploration of seven of the broad facets of this most basic forms of Christian literature. A chapter is devoted to each and relates that facet to all of the others. *978-157312-767-7 432 pages/pb* **$28.00**

If Jesus Isn't the Answer . . . He Sure Asks the Right Questions!
J. Daniel Day

Taking eleven of Jesus' questions as its core, Day invites readers into their own conversation with Jesus. Equal parts testimony, theological instruction, pastoral counseling, and autobiography, the book is ultimately an invitation to honest Christian discipleship. *978-1-57312-797-4 148 pages/pb* **$16.00**

I'm Trying to Lead . . . Is Anybody Following?
The Challenge of Congregational Leadership in the Postmodern World
Charles B. Bugg

Bugg provides us with a view of leadership that has theological integrity, honors the diversity of church members, and reinforces the brave hearts of church leaders who offer vision and take risks in the service of Christ and the church. *978-1-57312-731-8 136 pages/pb* **$13.00**

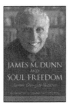

James M. Dunn and Soul Freedom
Aaron Douglas Weaver

James Milton Dunn, over the last fifty years, has been the most aggressive Baptist proponent for religious liberty in the US. Soul freedom—voluntary, uncoerced faith and an unfettered individual conscience before God—is the basis of his understanding of church-state separation and the historic Baptist basis of religious liberty.

978-1-57312-590-1 224 pages/pb **$18.00**

The Jesus Tribe
Following Christ in the Land of the Empire
Ronnie McBrayer

The Jesus Tribe fleshes out the implications, possibilities, contradictions, and complexities of what it means to live within the Jesus Tribe and in the shadow of the American Empire.

978-1-57312-592-5 208 pages/pb **$17.00**

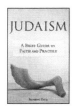

Judaism
A Brief Guide to Faith and Practice
Sharon Pace

Sharon Pace's newest book is a sensitive and comprehensive introduction to Judaism. How does belief in the One God and a universal morality shape the way in which Jews see the world? How does one find meaning in life and the courage to endure suffering? How does one mark joy and forge community ties? *978-1-57312-644-1 144 pages/pb* **$16.00**

Looking Around for God
The Strangely Reverent Observations of an Unconventional Christian
James A. Autry

Looking Around for God, Autry's tenth book, is in many ways his most personal. In it he considers his unique life of faith and belief in God. Autry is a former Fortune 500 executive, author, poet, and consultant whose work has had a significant influence on leadership thinking.

978-157312-484-3 144 pages/pb **$16.00**

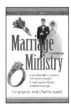

Marriage Ministry: A Guidebook
Bo Prosser and Charles Qualls

This book is equally helpful for ministers, for nearly/newlywed couples, and for thousands of couples across our land looking for fresh air in their marriages.   *1-57312-432-X 160 pages/pb* **$16.00**

Meeting Jesus Today
For the Cautious, the Curious, and the Committed

Jeanie Miley

Meeting Jesus Today, ideal for both individual study and small groups, is intended to be used as a workbook. It is designed to move readers from studying the Scriptures and ideas within the chapters to recording their journey with the Living Christ.

978-1-57312-677-9 320 pages/pb **$19.00**

The Ministry Life
101 Tips for Ministers' Spouses

John and Anne Killinger

While no pastor does his or her work alone, roles for a spouse or partner are much more flexible and fluid now than they once were. Spouses who want to support their minister-mates' vocation may wonder where to begin. Whatever your talents may be, the Killingers have identified a way to put those gifts to work.   *978-1-57312-769-1 252 pages/pb* **$19.00**

The Ministry Life
101 Tips for New Ministers

John Killinger

Sharing years of wisdom from more than fifty years in ministry and teaching, *The Ministry Life: 101 Tips for New Ministers* by John Killinger is filled with practical advice and wisdom for a minister's day-to-day tasks as well as advice on intellectual and spiritual habits to keep ministers of any age healthy and fulfilled.   *978-1-57312-662-5 244 pages/pb* **$19.00**

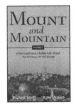

Mount and Mountain
Vol. 2: A Reverend and a Rabbi Talk About the Sermon on the Mount

Rami Shapiro and Michael Smith

This book, focused on the Sermon on the Mount, represents the second half of Mike and Rami's dialogue. In it, Mike and Rami explore the text of Jesus' sermon cooperatively, contributing perspectives drawn from their lives and religious traditions and seeking moments of illumination.   *978-1-57312-654-0 254 pages/pb* **$19.00**

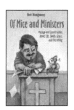

Of Mice and Ministers
Musings and Conversations About Life, Death, Grace, and Everything
Bert Montgomery

With stories about pains, joys, and everyday life, *Of Mice and Ministers* finds Jesus in some unlikely places and challenges us to do the same. From tattooed women ministers to saying the "N"-word to the brotherly kiss, Bert Montgomery takes seriously the lesson from Psalm 139—where can one go that God is not already there?   *978-1-57312-733-2 154 pages/pb* **$14.00**

Place Value
The Journey to Where You Are
Katie Sciba

Does a place have value? Can a place change us? Is it possible for God to use the place you are in to form you? From Victoria, Texas to Indonesia, Belize, Australia, and beyond, Katie Sciba's wanderlust serves as a framework to understand your own places of deep emotion and how God may have been weaving redemption around you all along.

978-157312-829-2 138 pages/pb **$15.00**

Preacher Breath
Sermon & Essays
Kyndall Rae Rothaus

"*Preacher Breath* is a worthy guide, leading the reader room by room with wisdom, depth, and a spiritual maturity far beyond her years, so that the preaching house becomes a holy, joyful home. . . . This book is soul kindle for a preacher's heart."   —Danielle Shroyer

Pastor, Author of *The Boundary-Breaking God*

978-1-57312-734-9 208 pages/pb **$16.00**

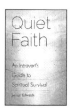

Quiet Faith
An Introvert's Guide to Spiritual Survival
Judson Edwards

In eight finely crafted chapters, Edwards looks at key issues like evangelism, interpreting the Bible, dealing with doubt, and surviving the church from the perspective of a confirmed, but sometimes reluctant, introvert. In the process, he offers some provocative insights that introverts will find helpful and reassuring.   *978-1-57312-681-6 144 pages/pb* **$15.00**

Reading Deuteronomy
(Reading the Old Testament series)
A Literary and Theological Commentary

Stephen L. Cook

A lost treasure for large segments of today's world, the book of Deuteronomy stirs deep longing for God and moves readers to a place of intimacy with divine otherness, holism, and will for person-centered community. The consistently theological interpretation reveals the centrality of this book for faith. *978-1-57312-757-8 286 pages/pb* **$22.00**

Reflective Faith
A Theological Toolbox for Women

Susan M. Shaw

In *Reflective Faith*, Susan Shaw offers a set of tools to explore difficult issues of biblical interpretation, theology, church history, and ethics—especially as they relate to women. Reflective faith invites intellectual struggle and embraces the unknown; it is a way of discipleship, a way to love God with your mind, as well as your heart, your soul, and your strength. *978-1-57312-719-6 292 pages/pb* **$24.00**

Workbook 978-1-57312-754-7 164 pages/pb **$12.00**

Sessions with Psalms (Sessions Bible Studies series)
Prayers for All Seasons

Eric and Alicia D. Porterfield

Useful to seminar leaders during preparation and group discussion, as well as in individual Bible study, *Sessions with Psalms* is a ten-session study designed to explore what it looks like for the words of the psalms to become the words of our prayers. Each session is followed by a thought-provoking page of questions. *978-1-57312-768-4 136 pages/pb* **$14.00**

Sessions with Revelation
(Sessions Bible Studies series)
The Final Days of Evil

David Sapp

David Sapp's careful guide through Revelation demonstrates that it is a letter of hope for believers; it is less about the last days of history than it is about the last days of evil. Without eliminating its mystery, Sapp unlocks Revelation's central truths so that its relevance becomes clear.

978-1-57312-706-6 166 pages/pb **$14.00**

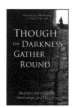

Though the Darkness Gather Round
Devotions about Infertility, Miscarriage, and Infant Loss

Mary Elizabeth Hill Hanchey and Erin McClain, eds.

Much courage is required to weather the long grief of infertility and the sudden grief of miscarriage and infant loss. This collection of devotions by men and women, ministers, chaplains, and lay leaders who can speak of such sorrow, is a much-needed resource and precious gift for families on this journey and the faith communities that walk beside them.

978-1-57312-811-7 180 pages/pb **$19.00**

Time for Supper
Invitations to Christ's Table

Brett Younger

Some scholars suggest that every meal in literature is a communion scene. Could every meal in the Bible be a communion text? Could every passage be an invitation to God's grace? These meditations on the Lord's Supper help us listen to the myriad of ways God invites us to gratefully, reverently, and joyfully share the cup of Christ.   978-1-57312-720-2 246 pages/pb **$18.00**

A Time to Laugh
Humor in the Bible

Mark E. Biddle

With characteristic liveliness, Mark E. Biddle explores the ways humor was intentionally incorporated into Scripture. Drawing on Biddle's command of Hebrew language and cultural subtleties, *A Time to Laugh* guides the reader through the stories of six biblical characters who did rather unexpected things.   978-1-57312-683-0 164 pages/pb **$14.00**

A True Hope
Jedi Perils and the Way of Jesus

Joshua Hays

Star Wars offers an accessible starting point for considering substantive issues of faith, philosophy, and ethics. In *A True Hope*, Joshua Hays explores some of these challenging ideas through the sayings of the Jedi Masters, examining the ways the worldview of the Jedi is at odds with that of the Bible.   978-1-57312-770-7 186 pages/pb **$18.00**

Word of God Across the Ages
Using Christian History in Preaching
Bill J. Leonard

In this third, enlarged edition, Bill J. Leonard returns to the roots of the Christian story to find in the lives of our faithful forebears examples of the potent presence of the gospel. Through these stories, those who preach today will be challenged and inspired as they pursue the divine Word in human history through the ages.   *978-1-57312-828-5 174 pages/pb* **$19.00**

The World Is Waiting for You
Celebrating the 50th Ordination Anniversary of Addie Davis
Pamela R. Durso & LeAnn Gunter Johns, eds.

Hope for the church and the world is alive and well in the words of these gifted women. Keen insight, delightful observations, profound courage, and a gift for communicating the good news are woven throughout these sermons. The Spirit so evident in Addie's calling clearly continues in her legacy.   *978-1-57312-732-5 224 pages/pb* **$18.00**

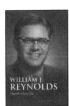

William J. Reynolds
Church Musician
David W. Music

William J. Reynolds is renowned among Baptist musicians, music ministers, song leaders, and hymnody students. In eminently readable style, David W. Music's comprehensive biography describes Reynolds's family and educational background, his career as a minister of music, denominational leader, and seminary professor.   *978-1-57312-690-8 358 pages/pb* **$23.00**

With Us in the Wilderness
Finding God's Story in Our Lives
Laura A. Barclay

What stories compose your spiritual biography? In *With Us in the Wilderness*, Laura Barclay shares her own stories of the intersection of the divine and the everyday, guiding readers toward identifying and embracing God's presence in their own narratives.

978-1-57312-721-9 120 pages/pb **$13.00**

Made in the USA
Charleston, SC
27 October 2015